D1551476

"BIOFEEDBACK, FASTING & MEDITA-
TION is truly an incredible book. It provides
an introduction to the theoretical underpinnings of biofeedback, fasting, and meditation
as well as an understanding of their interrelationship for us.

"Everything you always wanted to know (and
might not have thought of asking) is included
as well as a comprehensive survey of research
relating to each area. . . . All of this is placed
within the context of an understanding of the
human body. . . .

"This book may change your life. It did mine!"

Elayne J. Kahn, Ph.D.

BIOFEEDBACK,

FASTING

&

MEDITATION

**GARY and STEVE NULL
and Staff**

PYRAMID BOOKS
NEW YORK

BIOFEEDBACK, FASTING & MEDITATION

A PYRAMID BOOK

First printing November, 1974

ISBN: 0-515-03400-2

Library of Congress Catalog Card Number: 74-17725

Copyright © 1974 by Gary Null
All Rights Reserved

Printed in the United States of America

Pyramid Books are published by Pyramid Communications, Inc. Its trademarks, consisting of the word "Pyramid" and the portrayal of a pyramid, are registered in the United States Patent Office.

PYRAMID COMMUNICATIONS, INC.
919 Third Avenue
New York, New York 10022, U.S.A.

TABLE OF CONTENTS

FOREWORD

Biofeedback, Fasting and Meditation is truly an incredible book. It provides an introduction to the theoretical underpinnings of fasting, meditation and biofeedback as well as an understanding of their interrelationship and application for us. Everything you always wanted to know (and might not have thought of asking) is included. The potential of these approaches in offering self-help for health problems is included as well as a comprehensive survey and discussion of research relating to each area. Dozens of research reports ranging from historical studies to current findings are listed! All of this material is then placed within the context of an understanding of the human body and its functioning.

We are living in a time of unprecedented interest and exploration of the functioning and control of the human mind and body and especially their interrelationship. Current enthusiasm for fasting, meditation and biofeedback focuses on their potential use as procedures to achieve greater mind control which in itself offers exciting possibilities. In addition, there is the potential for using mind control to affect bodily functioning. The idea that the mind can be controlled has only recently gained acceptance within the scientific community. The relationship between the mind and the functioning of the human body has been even harder to accept. To be able, in this way, to control some of the most prevalent of the 20th century illnesses such as hypertension, migraine headaches, and anxiety is astounding. It should not be surprising, however, since these are the illnesses that have been most resistant to treatment by drugs and thought to be most closely related to emotional states.

This book may change your life. It did mine. The examination of long-held beliefs about the importance of eating and overeating in light of the value of fasting is shocking. You will undoubtedly feel as I did and want to close the book after Chapter 2 to begin fasting immediately. Don't. Read on. There is a great deal of important information following that will help you make intelligent choices.

ELAYNE J. KAHN, Ph.D.

INTRODUCTION

Fasting, the main subject of this book is, like meditation, its subsidiary one, a practice of considerable antiquity. By both of these techniques, human beings in various societies and at various times have attempted, for many different reasons, to control both their bodies and their minds. We will also discuss biofeedback, a new scientific technique which many claim to be capable of producing the same effects as meditation but at a considerably accelerated pace. It has unquestionably given us many new and valuable insights into brain and nerve functioning and has gone far to explore the actual physiological and neurological effects of meditation.

This book represents a new approach to the subjects it covers, as well as an introduction to contemporary research on fasting. Scientists are now making exciting discoveries in the fields of physiology, biology, biochemistry, medicine and other related fields. Many of the normal processes of our bodies were either unsuspected or entirely unknown to previous generations. Consider, for example, discoveries about the role of vitamins in metabolic functioning, including the recent discoveries of new vitamins; or the present state of our knowledge concerning brain functioning. To be sure, scientific discoveries have far-reaching effects, many of which are far from benign. Among the detrimental discoveries must be counted the pesticides and other crop sprays which have greatly contributed to the pollution of the environment and of our bodies. Pesticides, let alone their effects, were unknown to many previous writers on the subject of fasting, but therapeutic fasting can to a small degree cleanse the body of the toxins resulting from the pesticide contamination. Whatever the disasters and hardships faced by past generations, many stresses and anxiety-causing dilemmas of modern urban-industrial society were simply nonexistent then. Therefore, the advantages or disadvantages of such regimens as fasting and meditation must be considered from an entirely new viewpoint in many cases, and it may be for reasons different from those appropriate to previous times and states of society that either technique may be used.

By and large, even relatively recent books on the subject of fasting were written by natural hygienists or nutritionists who rarely used any available studies by competent medical sources as evidence for the advisability of fasting. The same also applies to meditation. Because we believe that the sort of problems—pollution, overcrowding, crises in food production—and the anxiety which these and other problems cause can be alleviated to some extent in their effects on the individual by fasting and meditation, we have felt it necessary to go directly to scientific research, using the most recent clinical evidence available as well as rereading the work done in the past. We have read literally thousands of medical and scientific papers and journals in order to translate their findings into ordinary language. We do not feel that a discerning person can be convinced of the wisdom of fasting or meditation if presented with shallow or one-sided evidence. This is why the bibliographies and chapter references in this book are of tremendous importance. We urge readers who are seriously concerned with matters of health to do follow-up reading and research. Each of the articles and books suggested in the bibliographies has been selected to provide a wide range of alternatives as well as corroborative research and opinions on the subjects covered in this book. However, the speed of scientific research and the slowness of the publishing process are likely to ensure that many new studies and some new evidence not covered in this book will have appeared by the time that this book is available and this, we hope, will also be borne in mind by the reader.

Neither fasting, nor meditation, nor the therapeutic and research use of biofeedback techniques can cure, like magic, all the ills known to humanity or even a particularly sizeable proportion of them. All, we believe, can help alleviate some of their effects at least upon the individual. It must be remembered that it is only now becoming clear just what our problems are and how they are caused. We are at the frontiers of new knowledge in many things, not least in what might seem to be the most basic knowledge, the functioning of our bodies and our minds and how inextricably interrelated they are. What actually occurs in the course of a normal day within the billions of cells which make up a human being, or, indeed, any other organism, is extraordinary and fascinating. The metabolic, chemical, physiological and psychological changes which occur during fasting or meditation are fascinating subjects in themselves. Considered very soberly in the light of present social and health problems, these two ancient approaches used in combination can be of great benefit to us all.

PART I

The Ancient Art of Fasting

CHAPTER 1

FASTING: PAST AND PRESENT

During a fast, an individual abstains either partially or completely from food for a period of time which may be as short as several hours or as long as several months. Medically speaking, whenever all previous food taken has passed through the digestive processes of the body and undergone assimilation by the cells, the body is in a fasting state. A fast may be undertaken for religious, philosophical or therapeutic purposes. All three reasons are of considerable historical antiquity although, of course, it is the therapeutic aspect of fasting with which this book is concerned. However, let us briefly examine the historical background of fasting, which is likely to interest both those persons advised to fast for medical reasons, as well as the concerned reader.

Historical Background

Whether it has been used for the purposes of ritual, as a discipline, as a means of strengthening mind and body, a way of drawing the community together or for seeking magical powers, the notion of abstinence from food has had profound psychological force. This is hardly surprising, for food is, after all, the most basic necessity of life. Among all the peoples of the world there have been few, if any, religious and ethical systems which have not at some time institutionalized the practice of fasting. Fasting periods still play a vital role in the religious life of many of the world's peoples. In Judaism several days of the year are set aside as total fasts, the best known of these being the Day of Atonement. On this day no food may be taken between sunrise and sunset. In the Christian calendar, Lent is traditionally a period when only certain foods can be eaten. During the Islamic days of Ramadan, food can only be taken in the evening. However, there is usually no restriction on what food may be eaten or in what quantities. Hindu yogic practice especially emphasizes both the spiritual and the nutritional values of regular periods of fasting.

For most religions, fasting must have started as a stern way of testing the individual or the group. Where the results of hunting were uncertain and crop failure was, and still is, a grim reality, periods of fasting enforced by the exigencies of nature might well turn into periods of famine when the excess tissues of the body are all used up and the organism, forced to feed on the vital tissues of the body organs, gradually starves. In large areas of the world, famine is a constant threat. Under such circumstances, fasting then has a particularly strong and awesome significance. For the more "primitive" religions whose members still live close to the earth, the beneficial aspects of fasting can also be quickly understood. Just as animals can be observed to go without food when they are sick, often first eating some herb which will cause them to vomit, the human appetite diminishes when it is of value to abstain from food. That we are less and less able, in modern, scientifically oriented society, to interpret our physical needs by such basic awareness is one of the problems of modern life. It is a mistake on the part of modern, urban, civilized people to believe that technology has so separated us from our animal state that the laws of nature no longer apply to us.

Religious fasting, however, has little or nothing to do with nutritional demands or the improvement of health. The major concern, especially in the Judeo-Christian world, has been with the disciplining of the body for the purpose of spiritual improvement.

Fasting in Ethiopia

Coptic Christian practice in Ethiopia is especially interesting not only because of the particular sternness of its rules concerning the enforcement of fasting, but also because of the extraordinarily large part of the year which fasts of various lengths occupy. It is estimated that for ordinary people the total number of fasting days amounts to something like 110 days of the year. For especially religious people and the clergy, the number of fasting days can reach the formidable number of 220. None of the fasts of the Coptic year are total in the sense that all nutrition is prohibited. Like the Islamic fasts—and of course Ethiopia is partly a Moslem country—actual abstinence covers only part of the day. After midday, the orthodox are permitted to eat but the diet is very restricted.

During the fasting periods, some lasting for one

day and others for longer periods, the most lengthy
an eight-week fast before Easter, the dietary rules
prohibit the eating of any animal products whatso-
ever. This includes meat, butter, milk and eggs, but
does not include fish, which is mostly very hard to
come by in any case. Although certain groups are
theoretically excused from fasting, these groups—
children under seven, pregnant women, the sick and
the elderly—rarely take advantage of this provi-
sion.

For the majority of Ethiopians the diet is largely
a vegetarian one and cannot be considered nutri-
tionally balanced. Protein values are necessarily
very low in a poor country. Thus, fasting is more of
a hardship for the wealthier members of the community, among whom the consumption of meat is
more frequent. However, although the protein content of the fasting diet is low, lower than that normally considered necessary for healthy survival, the
maximum amount possible is extracted from vegetables and certain seeds. Fenugreek, for instance,
which is a staple of the Ethiopian diet during both
fasting and non-fasting periods, is estimated to
contain between 20 and 23 percent protein. Other
typical foodstuffs eaten during both fasting and
non-fasting periods, include broad beans, safflower
seeds, and sunflower seeds. These are also good
sources of protein and calories. Sunflower seeds
contain about 16 to 20 percent protein.

The fasting diet of the Ethiopian Coptic church
raises many interesting nutritional questions. Although there are certain groups of the population
to whom fasting can be detrimental, particularly
young children, the majority of the population do
not show the sort of protein deficiencies that would
be expected by western standards of nutrition—at

any rate, not under normal, non-famine circumstances.

Therapeutic Fasting

The beneficial effects of fasting have been propounded for several thousand years. History is full of famous advocates of fasting and its medicinal advantages have long been praised in various cultures. A fasting cure for syphilis was recommended by the ancient Egyptians. Plato claimed that regular fasts improved both mental and physical capabilities, himself undertaking fasts of ten days at a time. Pythagoras likewise advocated fasting. His 40-day fast before sitting for an examination at the University of Alexandria is one of the better-known historical examples of fasting. Pythagoras was so impressed by the effects of his experience that he later required his own students to fast before commencing their studies with him.

Plutarch considered a day's abstinence from food to be far better than any medicine in dealing with ill health and Hippocrates prescribed fasts during the critical phases of an illness. The great Arab physician Avicenna recommended fasts of from 3 to 5 weeks to his patients while the sixteenth-century Swiss doctor Paracelsus proclaimed that fasting was the best possible remedy for all diseases.

With the sophistication of medical knowledge in the nineteenth century, fasting as therapy began to fall somewhat into disrepute. The little research that was conducted, mostly by natural hygienists and nutritional experts, concerned the effects of fasting on the system. It is true that earlier in this century many books and articles appeared on the benefits of fasting, but only relatively recently has a large body of research been published on the specific effects of fasting on the various organs, cells and metabolic functioning of the body. This is not to say that earlier research is valueless, but because much information concerning physiology was unavailable, the conclusions drawn by many earlier researchers relied very heavily on personal observation and to some extent lacked sufficient documentation. A full list of pioneer researchers such as Dewey, Benedict, Childe, Arnold Erhet, Tilden and Shelton and their works will be found in the bibliography.

Early Research on Fasting and Rejuvenation

Much of the early research on fasting and rejuvenation was done at the beginning of this century by such scientists as Huxley in England and Childe, Schulz, Kunde, and Carlson and their colleagues at the University of Chicago. Much work was done on the effects of inanition (total fasting) on simple organisms such as worms and insects and some most extraordinary results gave fairly conclusive proof of the rejuvenating capacities of long-term fasting at least among the simple subjects used. A criticism of research conducted in the U.S. is that many researchers have preferred to use animal subjects and draw conclusions from them about the likely effects of the same treatment on human subjects. However, some research on the rejuvenating effects of fasting on human beings gave less dramatic but fairly solid proof.

Among the earliest published research, experiments using flatworms are discussed in the book *Senescence and Rejuvenescence* published in 1915 by Childe, using as evidence his researches at the

University of Chicago. Childe had fasted a batch of elderly earthworms until they were reduced to their minimum possible size. He then allowed them to feed normally until they had regained their former sizes. The animals were observed to be remarkably rejuvenated, almost as if reborn. Another scientist who used worms as experimental subjects for fasting was the British biologist T.H. Huxley who used planaria worms. He isolated one planarian from a colony and fasted it periodically. Between fasts it was fed the same diet as the other worms, but it outlived them by 19 normal worm generations. Schulz at the University of Chicago was able to increase the life span of his hydra specimens from 1 to 15 years.

The results proved that, during the process of fasting, rejuvenation was caused by a decreased rate of metabolism, that is, the process by which the cellular tissues are built up. Among the lower animals this process yielded remarkable results. Work also done at the University of Chicago showed that similar, if far less marked rejuvenation of cellular tissues could occur in fasted human subjects. Researchers Carlson and Kunde of the Chicago physiology department placed one subject, a man of 40, on a fourteen-day fast, at the end of which his body appeared to be in a physiological condition normal to a youth of 17. In Kunde's opinion, because the man's weight had been reduced by something like 45 percent, approximately half of his body was, when restored to pre-fast weight, made of entirely new protoplasm. Tissues of the body not involved in the weight loss also, he believed, probably underwent a chemical change and subsequent rejuvenation. Here one might take note of the remarkably youthful appearance possessed by many practicing yogis who conduct numerous fasts. Lines and wrinkles become less marked in older people who fast, complexions become clearer and the eyes brighter.

The Cleansing Effects of Fasting

Much emphasis was placed by earlier advocates of fasting on the cleansing properties of a fast. They maintained that, because fasting placed the body in a state of physiological rest, the eliminative processes of the system could be repaired and improved, as the body will in fact excrete larger than normal amounts of waste material in the urine in the first few hours of fasting. Toxins and undigested matter which the body had accumulated would thus be disposed of and the entire system cleansed.

While this factor is an important one, the cleansing properties of fasting were in fact underestimated by those specialists whose works are still, by and large, the only ones available on the subject. Arnold Ehret, for example, whose *Rational Fasting* first appeared in 1926 and has recently been reissued, placed great stress on the necessity of ridding the body of mucus. However, the kinds of toxic substances which threaten the kidneys, liver and lower intestines in modern society were often nonexistent at the beginning of the century or, if they were known, their harmful properties were not evident. We speak, of course, of the toxic residues built up in the system by industrial and agricultural pollutants, especially of crop sprays which enter and contaminate foods and eventually poison the system itself, causing damage, much of which has only recently been discovered. For the fasting advocates of the early part of this century, the cleansing proc-

ess consisted of the elimination by the body of undigested foods.

Fasting and Disease

Usually early advocates of fasting presented their
findings in a blend of observation and conjecture
that contained little research of a truly scientific
and investigative nature. Nevertheless, some of the
statistical evidence they mention testifies to a certain amount of success in the treatment, by fasting,
of various conditions. Some of those conditions, for
instance, diseases of the heart and liver, hypertension, renal and gall bladder infections, arthritis and
varicose veins, have been proven by recent research
to respond by degrees to fasting. These diseases are,
of course, particularly common in the obese.

Whether diseases of the blood respond similarly
to fasting is not so clear. Nevertheless, some success
has resulted in dealing with diseases such as diabetes and other disorders of the glucose metabolism. Tilden, working before the First World War,
found that subjects suffering from pernicious anemia doubled their red blood count after a week of
fasting. Weger, writing in the late 1920's, reported
one case in which the hemoglobin of his patient increased by 50 percent and the white blood cells
were reduced by the same amount in the course of a
twelve-day fast. He also found that the excess
count of white blood cells produced in leukemia decreased during a fast. Other researchers testified
that other side effects of leukemia yielded to fasting
treatments. Unfortunately, these tentative sugges-
tions led to exaggerated claims that fasting was a
miracle cure for cancer. This sort of misrepre-
sentation is, of course, highly dangerous for, while

fasting certainly is a way of strengthening the body and enabling the individual to resist disease, there is no certain evidence that it can cure cancer or any other degenerative disease.

The suggestion, however, was and is an interesting one. B.A. MacFadden, for example, believed that the body could be compelled to absorb foreign growths if fasted long enough. His prognosis was that just as enzymes will digest the tissues of an abscess when it comes to the surface of the skin, so could they eliminate tumorous growths. Armstrong in England did report that female breast tumors could be seen to disappear during fasts of between four and 20 days' duration. James MacEachen, who supervised a total number of 715 fasts between 1952 and 1958 at his sanitorium in Escondido, California, also confidently reported that fasting cured cancer as well as high blood pressure, kidney disease, bronchitis, asthma, anemia, colitis and heart disease, and believed that the rate of complete recovery would have been higher if his patients had all been able to extend their fasts. Natural hygienist H.M. Shelton claimed that poliomyelitis responds well to fasting and believed that at least the suffering caused by multiple sclerosis could be alleviated through fasting. C.C. Clemmensen, using more thoroughly scientific methods than many of his colleagues, conducted 155 fasts on epileptic patients at the Hospital for Nervous and Mental Diseases in Denmark. In 1932, he published his findings that fasting effectively prevented epileptic attacks in the majority of cases within four or five days, whatever the previous history of the sufferers.

Fasting and Present Attitudes

Tremendous advances have been made over the last twenty years in scientific knowledge and scientific methodology. Paradoxically, those advances do not allow scientists the sweeping statements of former years concerning such things as the possible curative value of fasting. The workings of the human system have been shown to be even more intricate and complex than was suspected, and much of the research now being done on fasting produces only tentative conclusions about its therapeutic uses.

Fasting has been shown to have an effect on disease which is the reverse of most modern chemical specifics. While most modern medicines and drugs result in the suppression of symptoms, the purgative process of fasting tends to bring out the symptoms of sickness. When no disease is present, fasting acts as preventive therapy, greatly increasing the body's resilience and power to cure itself by creating conditions of physiological rest. Thus a person of normally good health might indeed be able to overcome the early stages of a minor disease while resting the usual functions of the body in the fasting process. But to prescribe fasting for a person in whom a degenerative disease had advanced beyond the initial stages and who had previously been treated with pain-killing drugs, radiation and surgery (all of which weaken the body) would be of dubious value.

The self-curing process of fasting is instinctive among wild animals and even domestic pets to some degree. A sick animal, whatever its species, usually withdraws to some quiet, private place, abstaining from all food and activity until, in the course of time, it has either recovered from its sickness or died of it. This must also have been the way with primitive peoples and still is among those groups which have not come too much in contact with the frequently dubious (to them) benefits of civilization. In these days science is beginning to realize the value of instinct and to explore, research and explain why and how practices such as fasting or meditation work.

There is as yet a great deal of further research to be done in the area of fasting and not all the results of the research which has been done are conclusive in any way. That it is beneficial in certain cases and under certain conditions has, however, been abundantly established, certain dangers notwithstanding. In the following chapters we will attempt to elucidate further, using some of the results of recent research.

Bibliography

Allen, E.N.—Control of Experimental Diabetes by Fasting and Total Dietary Restriction (*J. Exp. Med.,* 1920)

Ash, J.E.—The Blood in Inanition (*Arch. Inter. Med.,* July, 1914)

Bassler, A.—The Fasting Cure Answered (*Monthly Cycle and Medical Bulletin*)

Bean, C.H.—Starvation and Mental Development (*Psychol. Clin., 3,* 1908)

Benedict, F.G.—*The Influence of Inanition on Metabolism* (Washington: Carnegie Institution Publications, 1907)

Benedict, F.G.—*A Study of Prolonged Fasting* (Washington: Carnegie Institution Publications, 1915)

Bragg, P.C.—The Miracle of Fasting (*Health Science,* 1970)

Carlson, A.J.—*The Control of Hunger in Health and Disease* (Chicago: 1916)

Carlson, A.J.—Hunger, Appetite and Gastric Juice Secretion in Man During Prolonged Fasting (*Am. J. Physiol., 45,* 1918)

Carrington, H.—*Fasting for Health and Long Life* (Mokelumne Hill, California: Health Research, 1953)

Carrington, H.—*Vitality, Fasting and Nutrition* (New York: Rebman, 1908)

Childe, C.M.—*Senescence and Rejuvenescence* (Chicago: University of Chicago Press, 1915)

Clemmensen, C.C.—*Inanition and Epilepsy: Studies in the Influence of Inanition upon Epileptic Attacks* (Copenhagen: Levin and Munksgaard, 1932)

Dewey, E.H.—*The True Science of Living* (London: Henry Brill, 1895)

Dewey, E.H.—*The No-Breakfast Plan and the Fasting Cure* (London: L.N. Fowler, 1900)

de Vries, Arnold—*Therapeutic Fasting* (Los Angeles: Chandler, 1963)

Ehret, Arnold—*Rational Fasting* (Los Angeles: Ehret, 1926; New York: Beneficial Books, 1971)

Frazier, B.C.—Prolonged Starvation (*Monthly Journal of Medicine and Surgery,* Louisville, 1908)

Gordon, A.—Prolonged Fast (*Montreal Medical Journal, 36,* 1907)

Guelpa, A.—*Autointoxication and Disintoxication* (New York: Rebman)

Guelpa, A.—Starvation and Purgation in the Relief of Disease (*Br. Med. J., 21,* 1910)

Hazzard, L.B.—Fasting for the Cure of Disease (*Physical Culture,* 1910)

Hazzard, L.B.—*Scientific Fasting* (New York: Grant Publications, 1927)

Hill and Eckman—*Starvation Treatment of Diabetes* (Mokelumne Hill, California: Health Research)

Howe, P.E. and Hawk, P.B.—A Metabolism Study on a Fasting Man (*Proceedings Am. Soc. Bio. Chem. 31,* 1912)

Howe, P.E. and Hawk, P.B.—Nitrogen Partition and Physiological Resistance as Influenced by Repeated Fasting (*J. Am. Chem. Soc., 33,* 1910)

Howe, P.E. and Hawk, P.B.—On the Differential Leucocyte Count during Prolonged Fasting (*Am. J. Physiol., 30,* 1912)

Knuttson, Karl Eric and Selinus, Ruth—Fasting in Ethiopia: An Anthropological and Nutritional Study (*Am. J. Clin. Nutr., 23,* 7, 1970)

Langfield, H.S.—On the Psychophysiology of a Prolonged Fast (*Psychol. Monog., 16,* 1914)

McCoy. F.—*The Fast Way to Health* (Los Angeles: McCoy Publications, 1938)

MacEachen, J.—*Fasting for Better Health* (Escondido, Calif.: J.M. MacEachen, 1957)

MacFadden, B.A.—*Fasting for Health* (Los Angeles: MacFadden Publications, 1923)

Margulis, S.—Contributions to the Physiology of Regeneration *(J. Exper. Zoology, 7,* 1909)

Margulis, S.—*Fasting and Undernutrition* (New York: Dutton, 1923)

Meltzer, S. and Morris, C.H.—On the Influence of Fasting upon the Bacteriological Action of the Blood (*J. Exper. Med., 4,* 1889)

Meyers, A.W.—Some Morphological Effects of Prolonged Inanition (*J. Med. Research, 36,* 1917)

Minot, C.S.—Senescence and Rejuvenation (*J. Physiol., 12,* 1891)

Null, Gary and Staff—*Food Combining Handbook,* Chapter 9 (New York: Pyramid, 1973)

Oldfield, J.—*Fasting for Health and Life* (London: C.W. Daniel, 1924)

Paton, N.D. and Stockman, R.—Observations on the Metabolism of a Fasting Man (*Royal Society, Edinburgh, 4,* 1889)

Penny, E.—Notes on a Thirty Day Fast (*Br. Med. J., 1,* 1909)

Purinton, E.E.—*Philosophy of Fasting* (New York: Lust, 1906)

Sands, N.J.—Prolonged Fasting as a Factor in the Treatment of Acute Disease, with Special Reference to Affections of the Alimentary Canal (*N.Y. State J. Med., 4,* 1904)

Shelton, H.M.—*Fasting Can Save Your Life* (Natural Hygiene, 1964)

Sinclair, Upton—*The Fasting Cure* (Mokelumne Hill, Calif.: Health Research, 1955)

Stern, H.—*Fasting and Undernutrition in the Treatment of Diabetes* (New York: Rebman, 1912)

Sweet, M.P.—*Hints on Fasting Well* (Mokelumne Hill, Calif.: Health Research, 1956)

Szekely, E.B.—*The Therapeutics of Fasting* (Tecate: 1942)

Tilden, J.M.—*Criticisms of the Practice of Medicine* (1909)

Weger, G.S.—*The Genesis and Control of Disease* (Los Angeles: 1931)

CHAPTER 2

WHAT IS FASTING?

Much confusion exists over the difference between starvation and fasting. It may indeed seem cruelly ironic to be recommending regular habits of fasting at a time when an alarming pattern of food shortages and grain scarcity is emerging all over the world and when famine is becoming one of the world's major problems.

As the affluent countries of the West become more prosperous in comparison to their underdeveloped neighbors, their citizens demand food in greater quantities with a richer protein content. To what extent this factor actually influences worldwide distribution is, of course, a matter of argument. However, it is certain that in the West we eat too much. American eating habits exceed actual nutritional needs, especially with regard to meat protein. This is not to say that the average American eats particularly well by nutritional standards. On the contrary—people appear to eat with very little knowledge of their nutritional needs. Their meals are incorrectly balanced; their foods are improperly combined; they consume far too many foods containing dangerous chemical additives; they eat too quickly, too often and too much. Digestive problems are extremely common, as well as obesity and its associated diseases. High cholesterol intake due to fatty content of the diet is, some authorities believe, a factor in heart disease.

The majority of Americans are persuaded that it is absolutely vital to eat three hearty meals a day in order to survive and maintain good health. The idea of going without even one of these meals for any reason is regarded with suspicion. That a majority of people in this country eat too many calories can be demonstrated by the statistics for obesity, among various sectors of the population. It has been estimated that between 65 and 70 percent of American men, women and children are overweight. If those people who are critically overweight continue to consume three hearty meals a day, they may be inviting all sorts of health problems and an overall shortening of life expectancy. It is well established that obesity is related to heart disease, arterial hypertension, arthritis, and renal, pulmonary and hepatic disorders to name but a few.

In a society in which the old ritualistic-religious aspects of fasting have lost their force and therapeutic fasting is regarded with distrust on the whole, voluntary abstention from food still maintains a powerful hold on the public imagination when practiced for political ends. One example of this was Dick Gregory's lengthy fast to protest the Vietnam war. It is necessary to make a distinction between fasting and starvation as well as to describe then what the difference is: where a fast ends and starvation commences—a vital distinction to make.

Fasting and Starvation

It would be an oversimplification to state that starvation commences only when all the food reserves of the body have been used up, for a great deal depends on the nature of those food reserves. If an individual is severely malnourished previous to fasting, then he is surely to suffer ill effects. This is why careful preparation is necessary before beginning a fast (explained in Chapter 4). Other factors are also contributory, such as the subject's mental and emotional state, history of disease and metabolic and biochemical makeup and body weight. Researchers and some nutritional doctors (c.f. Alan Nittler's *A New Breed of Doctor*) have revealed that for some subjects vitamin and mineral supplements are essential when fasting.

During a fast, the body feeds on its own food reserves, starting with the fat or adipose tissue. In obese persons, adipose tissue may account for as much as 65 percent of the body's total weight. Even in a relatively thin individual 20 percent of total weight may be fat. Most of the food reserves which are not immediately needed for repair or burned as energy are stored in the adipose tissues as fat. Since fat theoretically can be stored in unlimited quantities, obese people are best able to withstand the rigors of fasting.

After the organism has withdrawn all possible nutrients from the adipose tissue, all other sources of excess food material in the muscle tissues, nonvital cells of the organs, the reserves of blood and water are tapped until they, too, have been used up. It is at this point that the process of fasting has been completed and, if it is not or cannot be broken, then starvation will set in.

Dangers of Starvation

With starvation, the body, deprived of all other sources of food, has no other recourse but to feed on its own vital parts. Slowly but irrevocably the vital cells of the heart, brain, liver, kidneys, pancreas and other organs of the body will be burned for energy until all the once-healthy tissue has been destroyed to maintain what remains. When the functions of the body have been damaged beyond repair by this process, death occurs.

The effects of progressive starvation are well known. Extreme emaciation and utter physiological degeneration rapidly ensue. Acute malnutrition often results in permanent mental impairment and is a major cause of mental deficiency in children. This has been found to be true under conditions of famine and intense poverty, but even short-term semistarvation and starvation cause some permanent damage. Evidence of this was found by U.S. medical researchers in examining ex-POW's more than 10 years after their World War II experiences of starvation and malnutrition. Nearly all the men were found to be suffering from similar symptoms —exhaustion, shortness of breath, depression, irritability, lack of motivation, nausea, poor vision, muscular cramps especially in the calf muscles, abnormal perspiration, edema, and insomnia.

Recognizable Symptoms of Fasting

Fasting, on the other hand, has little in common symptomatically with the effects of starvation. As an example consider fasting during hibernation. For as with animals during their long winter sleep, fasting human beings enter a period of physiological rest. Basal metabolism slows down to accommodate itself to the limited supplies of nourishment available from adipose tissue and other sources. The highly complex chemical changes which synthesize these food supplies into the material the cells need will be described in detail in the next chapter, as will the complementary processes that excrete waste materials, impurities and toxins.

The outward symptoms of the complex changes and processes that occur in the body during fasting manifest themselves in easily identifiable symptoms such as a coated tongue—this occurs almost immediately, and the clearance of the tongue is the most frequent sign that the fast is reaching or has already reached completion. Other common signs of elimination include the appearance of mucus in the stools and urine, offensive smell, and bad breath. These signs are especially prevalent if the faster is suffering from some disease. Other side-effects include giddiness, nausea, vomiting and sometimes mild fever. The temperature may drop below normal and the pulse rate become erratic. If the pulse rate continues to be erratic or the temperature remains particularly low or abnormally high for more than a few hours, fasting should be discontinued.

As a result of the need to conserve energy, some fasters may sleep a great deal during a lengthy fast. This, of course, varies according to the individual's ability to store energy. Some people and some hibernating animals store sufficient energy in the form of adipose tissue (fat) to maintain themselves without additional sleep and rest. Like other energy levels, sexual desire varies considerably during fasts, but in most people it is reduced or disappears altogether.

After the first few hours the bowels become inactive, but elimination continues through the urine, the mucous membranes, including the nose, and in skin sometimes in the form of eruptions. In women, elimination through the menses is common, and women who suffer from any congestion of the uterus or ovaries are likely to have irregular periods.

Weight is lost according to the amount of fat stored on the body. An overweight individual may lose between one and five pounds in weight a day for the first few days of fasting after which a weight loss of one or two pounds a day is more usual. Hunger, usually keen enough to cause stress for the first few days of the fast, generally becomes blunted as the enzymes adapt to the situation and the stomach, used to large meals, shrinks. After three days hunger is usually minimal and, generally speaking, by the fifth there is no hunger at all. It is the return of hunger, in fact, which is the surest indication that the fast is no longer necessary and should be terminated.

Psychological Symptoms of Fasting

The brain, which can only use glucose for energy, must use a substitute sugar for its needs. While this occurs, certain slight personality changes are likely. The first few days of fasting when hunger predominates are likely to be stressful and uncomfortable, but as the fasting period lengthens, always assuming that the patient is getting sufficient rest, a fairly common pattern is the emergence of mild euphoria mixed with irritability and often pronounced childlike behavior.

In this context, psychological tests conducted on a group of obese men by Wine, Crumpton and Drenick of the University of California at Los Angeles is of interest. Their findings showed, along with improved physical condition, improved mental condition despite easy irritability and incidents of depression. Psychological tests found the outward signs of stress to be superficial, relating to a tendency to become more emotionally open. A typical reaction on the part of many of the fasters was that they became behaviorally immature with tendencies to exhibit childlike and dependent behavior. The researchers relate that a few of the men became quite infantile. Other manifestations included an increasing demand for attention, self-centeredness, and in some a tendency to try to provoke trouble in the ward.

An interesting and unexpected factor was the improved performance of the subjects on psychological tests. These included tests of learning ability, memorizing ability and mental control—all the latter included work with digits and nonsense syllables—and tests of strength of grip and hand steadiness. The only one of these tests which showed impairment in many of the subjects was strength of grip. Improved performance on simple psychological tests could have been a function of practice and the desire for approval; however, the researchers consider the improvement a direct result of the weight loss, a function of improved physical health and the resulting enhancement of self-esteem.

All the subjects who volunteered to take part in the above tests were emotionally stable. Tests carried out on psychiatric subjects, also obese, showed some similar responses. The initial response to early hunger was anxiety, as in the other group of patients, which in some cases was extreme enough for the patients to refuse to continue in the experiment. Others, who were simply not sufficiently motivated to continue, also withdrew. However, the patients who continued to fast for the whole period (10 days) showed a similar tendency towards mild euphoria and optimism and obvious childlike behavior with irritable responses.

However, not all researchers have met with similarly satisfactory results in the treatment of the obese. Munro and Duncan of the Eastern General Hospital, Edinburgh, and the Royal Infirmary, Edinburgh, respectively, dispute the suitability of fasting therapy, at any rate short-term fasting for the obese, feeling that despite the extensive weight loss during the period of the fast, once the patient is eating normally again, all previous losses will be quickly regained, since, they argue, few chronically obese patients possess sufficient motivation or are sufficiently strong-minded to retain their weight loss outside the supervised situation. Their findings seem to indicate that most patients will become heavier after fasting, since many will discontinue recommended dieting. Thus they consider short-term fasting for obesity unjustifiable.

However, the majority of studies carried out on fasting for obesity subjected the volunteer patients to considerably longer periods of fasting than those reported by the Scottish doctors and met with far greater success. Motivation is, moreover, a strong determining factor in success.

Fasting and Obesity

While there is some dispute whether short-term

or long-term fasting will cure more successfully obese patients of overeating than conventional diet methods, the great majority of investigations have used obese volunteers who wished to alter their detrimental dietary habits.

The problems of the obese start with impaired metabolic function. This occurs when the greater part of the work of the body must be devoted to storing excess food in the form of fat. Digestion and assimilation processes tend to be impaired, and fatty deposits accumulate not only in the adipose tissue but around organs, in some cases infiltrating the cells, especially of the liver, pancreas and heart. Thus, the diseases of the obese are multiple, primarily associated with the heart, liver, kidneys, with impaired functioning of the arteries through fatty deposits, and with hypertension (raised blood pressure).

Obesity and Hypertension

Although there is some dispute concerning the causes of hypertension, the tendency of most authorities is to believe that obesity is the major cause of this condition. The American Heart Association considers obesity to be the highest single cause of hypertension followed by excessive nervous tension, the stress factor. Stress is often linked behaviorally to obesity because certain personality types indulge in compulsive eating when suffering from nervous stress. Evidence for both these factors as causes of hypertension is fairly well documented (see Bibliography).

One of the best-known studies into the causes of hypertension is the study conducted at Framingham, Massachusetts, from 1949 onwards, which found that overweight people are more likely to be hypertensive. It was discovered that, as stored fat increased, blood pressure also increased. Another finding was that thin subjects who became hypertensive then developed a tendency towards obesity. A significant proof of the link between obesity and hypertension was that when overweight people were able to reduce their weight as they were advised to do, their blood pressure levels also went down. This was true of about 60 percent of the Framingham hypertension sufferers who were able to lose sufficient weight.

Another study which supports the evidence of obesity-induced hypertension was carried out at the University of Alabama Medical School by Harlan and his colleagues. This study, which extended over thirty years, used as subjects one thousand prospective candidates for naval flight training and was carried out in cooperation with the U.S. Naval Aerospace Medical Research Institute. The study was initiated in 1940, at which time the subjects were all aged 24. Throughout the years of the study, frequent follow-up examinations were conducted, revealing that approximately half the men were suffering from high blood pressure and that in most cases these men were also overweight. The major weight increases seemed to occur between the ages of 24 and 36 and in the majority of cases it was during this period that their blood pressure levels started their dangerous rise.

It has been estimated that approximately 24 million Americans suffer from hypertension. This figure, in itself grave, is rendered even more serious by the fact that many subjects who were screened for hypertension were unaware that they suffered from the condition. Hypertension is, in fact, far more common than cancer, yet receives comparatively scant attention. So much ignorance surrounds the condition that in many cases it is only after a sufferer has fallen victim to a stroke or some other serious disease that the condition becomes apparent. By that time, it is often too late. Hypertension is the greatest single contributory factor in several types of heart disease such as angina pectoris, myocardial infarction, and arteriosclerosis—hardening of the arteries of the heart, brain and limbs often leading to cerebral hemorrhage, fatty degeneration of the liver, kidney failure as well as degenerative diseases of the vision and premature aging.

Compared to normal, healthy people, obese men and women show a greater tendency for heart disease, cerebral hemorrhage, and chronic nephritis, a kidney disease.

Diabetes and Obesity

Another disease which appears to be alarmingly on the increase is diabetes. There seems to be some connection between obesity and diabetes as well as other malfunctions of sugar metabolism. In diabetes, the peripheral tissues such as those of skeletal muscles exhibit an inability to properly metabolize glucose. Production and secretion of the hormone insulin is insufficient and since obesity increases basal insulin needs, the likelihood of diabetes increases with extra bulk, especially if the patient has a tendency towards impaired glucose metabolism.

Dangers of Fasting

Although fasting has many advantages, much

more is also known today about its disadvantages and dangers. Fasting is most commonly recommended as a weight-reducer in chronic obesity and as a purgative to cleanse the body of toxins and poisons which are the by-products not only of faulty digestion but of industrial pollutants and food additives.

Fasts performed as one-shot cure-alls may be traumatic psychologically, if not physiologically. But, on the whole, regularly performed fasts seem to be desirable for obese people who do not suffer from renal (kidney) failure. The sort of diets prescribed to overweight people often impose a strain on the patient because he is always hungry. The high protein, low carbohydrate diet usually recommended to the overweight may be harmful if carbohydrate metabolism is impaired, as it often is in obese people. Once initial weight has been lost and the metabolic defects hopefully corrected, this sort of diet has more possibility of success. All in all, so long as strict precautions are observed, fasting would seem to be the best method to correct such defects and prepare for dieting.

Although there is much evidence to justify fasting for obesity, there are potential dangers in fasting for other conditions. Some authorities are convinced that during a fast such toxins as insecticides (stored in fatty tissue) as well as additives and other pollutants, including lead, can be extremely dangerous if released too quickly into the bloodstream. When this happens the 'faster' can literally poison himself, which might lead to severe illness, even death. This sudden release of poisons can be stemmed by taking juices or selected fruits to dilute the concentration of toxic substances being eliminated. Others feel that electrolytes, vitamins, particularly the water soluble fractions, as well as valuable proteins and minerals are also lost. This is why the more enlightened nutritional doctors supply these supplements during a fast so that the body can maintain health while being detoxified. In the majority of cases, all of the bodily functions in the re-fed individual will be greatly improved and invigorated in response to the detoxifiying effect of fasting.

The following chapters will deal a little more extensively with the effects which fasting has on the body and give some advice on the method of carrying out a fast. However, we would advise the reader who lacks extensive knowledge of physiological and biochemical functioning that, before embarking on a fast for the first time, he should seek a physician's advice and supervision.

Bibliography

American Heart Association—*Heart Facts 1972*

Anon.—Epidemiological Assessment of the Role of Blood Pressure in Stroke: Framingham Study (*J.A.M.A., 214,* 1970)

Barhydt, Frank—Fasting: Therapy or Folly? (*Let's Live,* July 1972)

Consolazio, C. Frank et al.—Metabolic Aspects of Acute Starvation in Normal Humans (*Am. J. Clin. Nutr.,* 20, 7, 1970)

Crumpton, Evelyn et al.—Starvation: Stress or Satisfaction? (*J.A.M.A., 196,* 5, 1966)

Kahn, Harold A.—Change in Serum Cholesterol Associated with Changes in the U.S. Diet 1909-1965 (*Am. J. Clin. Nutr., 23,* 7, 1970)

Kalkoff, R.K. and Kim, H.H.—Metabolic Responses to Fasting and Ethenol Infusion in Obese Diabetic Subjects (*Diabetes, 22,* May 1973)

Lawler, T. and Wells, D.G.—Fasting as a Treatment of Obesity (*Postgrad. Med. J.,* June 1971)

Maagoe, H. and Mogensen, J.—The Effect of Treatment on Obesity (*Danish Med. Bull., 17, 7, 1970*)

Munro, I.F. and Duncan, L.J.P.—Fasting in the Treatment of Obesity (*The Practitioner, 208*, April 1972)

Silverstone, J.T. et al.—Hunger during Total Starvation (*Lancet,* July 18, 1966)

Sletten, Ivan W. et al.—Total Fasting in Psychiatric Subjects: Psychological, Physiological and Biochemical Changes (*Canad. Psychiat. Assoc. J., 12,* 1967)

Chapter 3

HOW FASTING AFFECTS
THE BODY

The process by which the body digests and absorbs food, assimilates it into the cells and converts some of it into energy and some into adipose tissue, or fat, is an extremely complicated process. The body is a factory for the conversion of food into energy which in turn is required to build up the tissues of the body, the bone, muscle, cartilage, nerve tissue, brain cells, organs, the blood circulatory system of veins, arteries and the heart, the respiratory system connected by the lungs. Animals, from the simplest protozoa to the most complex of the mammals, Man, derive this energy from food. All life is involved in eating. The basic form of food lies in the green plant which is either eaten directly or eaten by animals who in turn are eaten.

Plants use the energy of the sun to convert the simple molecules of oxygen, carbon dioxide and water into the more complex molecules which combine in various ways to form the different categories of food.

Food is combined into three main types of material, which are also the three main constituents that make up the body. They are called (1) carbohydrates (2) fats or lipids and (3) proteins, and all these materials are formed from the simple molecules of carbon, hydrogen and oxygen. Proteins, in addition, contain nitrogen. Nearly half the body is composed of protein, which is the half that is not composed of water in the form of intracellular and extracellular fluids. Protein is used in the building and repair of body cells (which are largely made up of protein), while carbohydrates and lipids provide energy and protective warmth. But, in order for these functions to be carried out, foods must be broken down by the process of digestion, which is aided by the catalyzing agents called enzymes and then further broken down and assimilated with the aid of another set of catalysts, the vitamins and minerals.

Fasting Metabolism

Fasting, the process of not eating, requires the body to go through a series of complex changes in order to continue to supply the system with enough energy to keep it functioning. Most of this "fuel" comes from the stored tissues of fat. Protein supplies need to be retained as long as possible since, once used, protein can only be replaced by more protein, not synthesized from other material. Glucose cannot be stored in the body during fasting. Instead, it must be synthesized partly from fat, partly from proteins, for the use of body tissues. This is why fasting is an easier process for the obese, in whom a greater quantity of fat is available.

Weight Loss

Loss of weight is the most obvious outward result of fasting. The greatest amount of weight is lost during the first ten days, the amount varying according to how much body water and fat is stored by the individual. Most fasting subjects lose between 1½ and 3 pounds over the first 24 hours and then about two pounds during the next 10 days after which the amount lost drops until, at the end of the second month, weight becomes stabilized for the duration of the fast. Ernst J. Drenick of the UCLA School of Medicine observed the weight loss of one obese subject who was fasted for over two months. Starting out at 540 pounds, the patient in question lost 71 pounds during the first month and 40 pounds in the second. Another patient whose prefasting weight was 230 pounds, lost 35 pounds in one month. The lighter the person initially, then the smaller the amount of weight lost.

The first ten or so days of fasting produces initially heavy weight losses, the composition of which is mostly water. Next in quantity after water come protein and fat loss.

Water and Mineral Losses

Sodium

Water is lost mainly through its transportation function since minerals are being excreted in the urine. Sodium loss is particularly heavy in the first 10 days. It is believed that sodium losses are due to salt deprivation and to the process of acidosis. However, it was found that fasting subjects lost more sodium in their urine than patients fed on a saltless diet. This may be because the fasting system handles sodium in a different way than the non-fasting system. Further evidence of this is given by the fact that, when fasters received sodium supplements, sodium was not excreted through the kidneys, but, when fasting subjects were re-fed with small amounts of carbohydrates, sodium excretion immediately became normal. Sodium loss, though it decreases over the course of the fast, also tends to fluctuate, and researchers are not in agreement about how or why so much sodium is excreted. Vervebrants and Arkay of Harvard Medical School think sodium excretion is an indication of the amount of sodium which is filtered by the kidneys during fasting and that some of this is perhaps reabsorbed. Runcie wonders if it may not be connected with another frequent result of fasting, the fall of blood pressure.

Potassium

Another important mineral which is lost in large amounts in the early days of fasting is potassium. The average loss of potassium of patients in one study was between 36 and 57 mEq (Milliequivalents—a special measurement for electrolytes such as potassium) at the onset of fasting, but this high level decreased during the first month to between 2.5 and 9.2 mEq. The patients in this group had received no potassium supplementation and were compared with another group who had been receiving a pre fasting low-calorie diet containing about 30 mEq of potassium. For this group the potassium loss during the first few days of fasting averaged about 17.8 mEq a day. Another group of patients in this University of California study were fed a supplement of 2 grams of potassium daily. Their initial potassium excretion was higher and decreased more slowly than that of the other two groups but, after 15 days, potassium intake was larger than its loss through urinary excretion. The patients who showed the lowest excretory amounts of potassium had been given potassium supplements both before and during the fast.

Another problem concerning loss of these minerals during fasting is that they appear to be adversely complementary. For instance, when sodium supplementation is given, an increase in potassium excretion occurs. This is a common phenomenon of the sodium-potassium balance usually controlled by Vitamin B_6.

Importance of Minerals

Deficiency or excessive loss of potassium may lead to muscular weakness, a frequent incident during fasting. Difficulty in concentrating is another associated problem. More serious problems concerning potassium deficiency are hypotension (low blood pressure) with impaired renal (kidney) function and respiratory problems. An excess of potassium causes the disease hyperkalaemia, which may produce muscular paralysis and damage the heart. It is caused by the transfer of potassium from the intracellular to the extracellular fluids.

A decrease in serum sodium levels causes dehydration, since a large volume of water is necessary to carry sodium out of the body. This can cause renal failure when severe. Low blood pressure and adrenal dysfunction may also result. Sodium deficiency can also cause fatigue.

Other Minerals

As with sodium and potassium, all mineral excretion during fasting tends to be excessive. The excretion of nitrates and other minerals is considered by Consolazio and others to result from dehydration and the depletion of protein stored by the body. They conclude that carbohydrate metabolism is inseparable from the metabolism of water and minerals. Mineral loss, which can affect health seriously, is prevented by some alert doctors who supply fasters with minerals.

Protein Loss

During fasting, very little carbohydrate is stored. Therefore, glucose has to be synthesized from fat and protein by the process of glucoeogenesis, to be further converted into energy for the central nervous system. In the initial stages of fasting about 75 grams of protein a day are lost, but this amount decreases to between 18 and 24 grams a day. The total amount of lean protein tissue used by the body for catabolism (metabolism which involves the release of energy), although far less than the fat, unfortunately may have some deleterious effects on the body, such as hair loss and dry skin. Normally hair will grow back when fasting is completed. However, Rooth and Carlstrom, two Swedish research scientists, consider it advisable to supplement fasting patients with small amounts of protein.

Vitamin Excretion

Vitamins of the B group (which are water soluble) have been found to be excreted in very large quantities in the early days of fasting by some subjects. According to Swendseid and others, fasting subjects were unable to utilize vitamin supplements as effectively as other researchers have claimed. Of the vitamins of the B complex, Vitamin B_6 (pyridoxine) seems to be excreted in quantities which cause a defficiency, while the excretion of riboflavin, pantothenic acid and biotin decreased as fasting continued.

Acidosis

Metabolic acidosis is the result of a lowering in bicarbonate and carbon values in the blood and is caused by renal failure to secrete sufficient hydrogen, excretion of bicarbonate (HCO_3) and an increase in the production of ketoacids. It causes the urine to become highly acid.

Acidosis generally develops within 5 days after fasting starts. If the subject does not develop acidosis, or if it suddenly clears, this can be taken as a sign that the fast has been broken. Much of the weight lost during fasting is due in part to acidosis and the accompanying fluid losses, which are heavy while the body is adapting to the acidosis. Sheila K. Ross and others found that even where potassium supplements were given, no significant drop in acidosis occurred. Ross and her colleagues do not favor fasting, because of the danger of kidney malfunction, which acidosis can cause.

On the other hand, Murphy and Zelman consider

acidification of the urine to be beneficial in helping to combat diseases of the urinary tract. To increase the acid content of urine they used ascorbic acid and compared the results against the urine of a group of fasting patients. They found that the total acid excretion of patients treated with ascorbic acid was between 65 and 85 mEq in 24 hours. Fasting patients tested at the same time had a total acid excretion of 131 mEq on average. A third group of patients, who had combined fasting with ascorbic acid, showed variable results of total acid excretion. In some patients the acid levels were lower, in others much higher, one patient for instance excreting 163 mEq in 24 hours.

Similar results were found when the ammonium content of the urine was measured. Ascorbic acid caused an excretory output of between 41 and 58 mEq of ammonium and fasting patients' ammonium increased to 79 mEq. They found that the administration of ascorbic acid diminished sodium excretion, although it left potassium excretion unchanged. The solubility of calcium in the urine was also improved. On the whole, acidosis was increased with the advantage that the Ph (acid/base metabolism) of blood did not change.

Carbohydrate Metabolism

During fasting, the body becomes less able to tolerate glucose, as is demonstrated by ketosis and a diabetes-like condition affecting oxidation. The carbohydrate intolerance is thought to be caused by the activity of contra-insulin hormones such as plasma-growth hormone, which increases during fasting. With prolonged fasting, insulin secretion is lowered and glucogen levels raised. Serum concentration of free fatty acids also appears to cause glucose intolerance. The enzymes employed in gluconeogenesis of the liver are also thought to contribute to glucose intolerance, as is the action of the hormone epinephrine on liver and adipose tissue.

According to Misbin and others the peculiarities of carbohydrate metabolism during fasting are due to the fact that the autonomic nervous system is controlling the glucose metabolism. These researchers feel that the emotional stress which can cause ketosis in diabetes may also be responsible for the overproduction of ketones in fasting. This is an interesting field of study which does not seem to have been investigated previously. Most authorities consider hormones to have the most important role in the chemical changes which occur in fasting. They see irregularities in carbohydrate metabolism as a result of the system's effort to preserve fasting protein levels as far as possible.

A great deal more work is still to be done before we can be absolutely sure how the various metabolic and hormonal changes which occur in fasting influence each other. On the whole, it seems that most of the problems can be countered with the supplementation of small quantities of those minerals and vitamins which the body excretes most heavily to protect the body while fasting.

Bibliography

Bloom, W.L. et al.—Comparison of Metabolic Changes in Fasting Obese and Lean Patients (*Ann. N.Y. Assoc. Sci.*, *131*, 1965)

Clark, Linda—*Get Well Naturally* (New York: Arco Books)

Consolazio, C. Frank et al.—Metabolic Aspects of Caloric Restriction: Nitrogen and Mineral Balance and Vitamin Excretion (*Am. J. Clin. Nutr.*, August 21, 1968)

Drenick, Ernst J. et al.—Body Potassium Content in Obese Subjects and Potassium Depletion during Prolonged Fasting (*Am. J. Clin. Nutr.*, April 18, 1966)

Drenick, Ernst J.—Weight Reduction by Prolonged Fasting (*Med. Times, 100,* 1, 1972)

Mahler, R.J. and Szabo, Olga—Studies in the Mechanism of Carbohydrate Intolerance Produced by Fasting (*Metabolism, 19,* April 1970)

Misbin, Robert L. et al.—Adrenergic Regulation of Insulin Secretion during Fasting in Normal Subjects (*Diabetes, 19,* October 1970)

Murphy, Francis J. and Zelman, Samuel—Ascorbic Acid as a Urinary Acidifying Agent; 1: Comparison with Ketogenetic Effect of Fasting (*J. Urol., 4,* September 1965)

Nittler, Alan—*A New Breed of Doctor* (New York: Pyramid, 1974)

Rooth, G. and Carlstrom, S.—Theraupeutic Fasting (*Acta Med. Scand., 187,* June 1970)

Ross, Sheil K. et al.—Blood/Acid Base Studies and Urinary Acid Excretion in Obese Fasting Patients (*Postgrad. Med. J., 47,* June 1970)

Runcie, J.—Urinary Sodium and Potassium Excretion in Fasting Obese Subjects (*Br. Med. J., 2,* April 1972)

Schroeder, Francis X. and Stinebaugh, B.J.—Studies on the Naturesis of Fasting: Relationship to Acidosis (*Metabolism, 15,* 1966)

Swendseid, M.E. et al.—Vitamin Excretion Studies in Starving Obese Subjects (*Am. J. Clin. Nutr., 4,* April 1967)

Verdy, Maurice and Champlain, Jacques de—Fasting in Obese Females (*Canad. Med. Assoc. J., 98,* June 1968)

Vervebrants, Egils and Arkay, Ronald A.—Effects of Fasting and Refeeding; 1: Studies on Sodium, Potassium and Water Excretion on a Constant Electrolyte and Fluid Intake (*J. Clin. Endochrin. & Metab., 29*, June 1969)

Vinyard, Elizabeth et al.—Vitamin B$_6$ Nutriture Studied in Obese Subjects during Eight Weeks of Starvation (*Am. J. Clin. Nutr.*, April 4, 1967)

Weinsier, R.L.—Fasting: A Review with Emphasis on the Electrolytes (*Am. J. Med., 50*, February 1971)

CHAPTER 4

THE EFFECTS OF FASTING ON THE BRAIN

Without sugar, the brain cannot function. That is to say: the main source of energy for the entire body comes from sugar, but while all the other organs of the body can use other food sources when glucose is unavailable, the brain for some reason can only metabolize glucose for energy. This is partly why the brain, although occupying only about 2½ percent of the total body weight, needs to use about a quarter of the sugar which is carried by the blood throughout the body. Other parts of the body are able to utilize fat for energy when insufficient carbohydrate-sugar is available. If the brain is deprived of sugar (as it is in fasting), it falls back on a substitute form of glucose. It has been discovered that the substrate used is made up of two organic acids known as ketones, or ketone bodies, that can be oxidized in combination with other substances to provide vital energy for the brain.

Before going on to describe this process as it occurs during fasting, it might be useful to look at the complex process by which sugar is utilized by the body and the brain.

Sugar Storage

The food sources for glucose are provided mainly by carbohydrates, by sugars and starches. Approximately 56 per cent of protein is also capable of being converted into glucose. Unfortunately, unlike fat, which can be stored in indefinite quantities as adipose tissue, glucose can only be stored to last for approximately four hours. Most of the glucose which is destined to be stored enters the liver, where some of the carbohydrates which have been ingested during the day are turned into glycogen and glucose. While glucose is providing the cells of the body with fuel to be burned immediately as energy, only a small quantity of it can be stored in the liver for later conversion into glycogen. Some of the proteins ingested during the day can be broken down into glycogen also and this protein-based glycogen gradually filters into the liver between meals. It is stored there until needed by the blood, at which time it, too, will be converted into glucose. However, in order for this process to occur, energy must already be available, and it can only be provided if sugar has already been burned. That is, energy is necessary to effect the conversion of protein into sugar first when it is stored in the liver and then when it is sent out to the blood as glucose.

Cellular Respiration

The glucose which is carried to the brain by the

blood is oxidized by the cells of the brain during a process which is known as cellular respiration. This is an immensely complicated process in which energy is formed from glucose after it has been burned down into a series of other substances called intermediates, each of which is essential for the formation of the next one in the chain. One of these intermediate substances is acetate, otherwise known as acetyl coenzyme A. It is considered to be the most important because it provides about 80 percent of the energy which is needed by the cells, but in reality it is only one of an interlocking chain and would be useless without the presence of the others. However, in order for the cells to be provided with sufficient energy, nearly all foods need to be chemically broken down into acetates.

The richest source of acetate is fat. Fat makes proportionally three times as much acetate as does sugar and twice as much as protein. Although the brain can only use glucose for energy, it can indirectly utilize fat in its intermediate acetate form. Fat, which is turned into acetate in the liver, only gains indirect access to the brain, for the acetate of fat is first carried to the other tissues of the body by the bloodstream.

The formation of glucose into acetates is carried out by the activity of other intermediate substances, of which there are many, including certain enzymes and vitamins. These are formed during the process of cellular respiration as it creates cycles of energy. The energy cycles are initially formed when a substance called adenosine triphosphate or ATP is released to form two specific cycles, namely the citric acid and the glycolysis cycles. Again, either these energy cycles will not be formed or their occurrence will be impaired if glucose is not being broken down at the same time to provide the initial energy to enable further energy cycles to take place.

In the course of the glycolytic cycles, a substance called pyruvate is formed. Pyruvate then is oxidized into O-acetate, which is the acetate of glucose. When this type of acetate combines with citric acid, the second cycle of energy will be formed. It is during the course of the citric acid cycles that the greatest quantity of energy is released. In the citric acid cycle, the substance known as adenine is an essential one.

Vitamins and Brain Function

A number of vitamins are essential to the energy-producing capacity of the brain cells. Unfortunately we do not always know the minimum quantities of certain of these key vitamins which are necessary for adequate functioning. This is true in the case of one of the most important members of the B-complex group, pantothenic acid. Although it is believed that the average balanced diet contains pantothenic acid in the amount of 10 milligrams a day, we do not know if this is sufficient. The importance of this vitamin was shown by experiments in which rats were deprived completely of pantothenic acid and the level of acetate in their cells dropped by 40 percent as a result. A deficiency in another member of the B-complex group, niacin, appears to slow down the brain's metabolic rate and, if this condition becomes severe, mental deterioration will result. All the B vitamins are vital for healthy functioning of the brain. Vitamin B_1 is essential for correct functioning of the heart and nervous system as well as the brain. Vitamin B_2 is needed by the nervous system. A lack of sufficient quantities of B_6 (pyridoxine) sometimes causes convulsions through impairment of nervous function, and B_{12} (cyancobalamin) is necessary for the production of red blood cells and platelets. A deficiency of B_{12} will cause pernicious anemia, brain and nerve damage.

Individuals differ in their needs for vitamins, according to their rate of metabolism or the speed at which oxidation takes place in the cells. Even an almost infinitesimal deficiency of a certain vitamin can affect the health profoundly. This is true in the case of some vitamins when excessive quantities have been built up. Too much Vitamin A, for instance, can cause mental disturbances and also damage to skin and bones, nausea and vomiting. Excessive Vitamin D can be responsible for the production of calcium in such abnormally high amounts that it will lead to kidney malfunction and also cause depressive states.

Deficiencies or excess states of vitamins are not always due to a diet which can be immediately labelled as helpful or unacceptable. The fact is that the dietary needs of individuals are not all alike; they vary according to the physiology of each person. This is extremely important to understand when investigating all the possible causes of a particular illness.

Sugar and the Brain

It is similarly true that different quantities of sugar are needed by different individuals. For instance, the oxidation of sugar will take place at slightly different rates, and these rates govern the amount of sugar needed and the rate at which energy is produced. If the brain oxidizes sugar faster than normal, acetate will be burned for energy at a faster rate and it will be necessary to reduce carbohydrate intake to maintain a correct balance. For other people, the brain oxidizes sugar too slowly and this can perhaps be corrected by cutting down on the amounts of proteins and fats.

It is very important to maintain a balanced level of brain sugar. For instance, a diet which is too low in carbohydrates may ensure that the brain only receives half the amount of sugar that it needs. Not only will there be an insufficient supply of glycogen in the liver, but its absence will also prevent protein conversion into sugar. A high carbohydrate diet will cause too high an intake of blood sugar by the brain, and this condition is also hazardous. Too high an intake of fat in the diet can slow down brain function. This occurs because excess fat-acetate cannot be utilized without a comparable amount of glucose O-acetate being present. (However, a too low fat intake can be disastrous in cold climates where additional fat is necessary to maintain body temperature. This is the reason that the Eskimo have a particularly fat-rich diet.) Fat is also necessary for assimilation of the fat-soluble vitamins A, E, D, and K.

Ketosis

The ketone bodies which the brain utilizes for glucose metabolism are made of two alcohol substances of the acetone type which are united by the triglycerides. Their production in large quantities during fasting in order to stimulate acetoacetate production by the liver is thought by Foster to be due to hyperactivation by the acetoacetate-synthesizing enzymes of the liver produced in the depression of insulin production by the pancreas. During fasting, ketone bodies are produced in excessive quantities, although no one has discovered why. Most theories claim that during fasting, the liver increases the rate at which free fatty acids drawn from peripheral food deposits are activated to acetyl coenzyme A. Another theory of ketosis maintains it is caused by the rate of synthesis, as opposed to oxidation of fatty acids.

During the course of the fast, ketosis gradually increases in response to the demands of the brain. Unfortunately it interferes with uric acid clearance, though the mechanism by which this occurs is not understood. In order to prevent further interference, the administration of either glucose or insulin will reverse the process of ketosis within five minutes.

According to one authority, one way the brain adapts to using ketone glucose is by absorbing B-Hydroxybutyrate. Where glucose uses up about 29 percent of brain oxygen, B-Hydroxybutyrate, just one of the substrates involved in ketosis, takes up about 52 percent of available oxygen. It is surprising that the brain is able to adapt to this type of gluconeogenesis as readily as it does, but this does explain the occasionally impaired brain functioning and mild euphoria associated with fasting.

Drenick and others carried out a study to discover whether the brain's adaptation to ketones during the fasting period was complete enough to resist the ill effects of glucose deficiency or whether the introduction of insulin could interfere with cerebral activity. Nine subjects were treated with insulin. Before fasting, they experienced the usual responses to insulin, ranging from nervousness to mental confusion. After the fast, the same subjects had no such reactions. As the effect of insulin on the blood is to lower sugar content, Drenick and his colleagues assumed that, during fasting, the brain did adapt to the small quantity of glucose available by utilizing ketones efficiently.

Genuth, in a study on diabetic and non-diabetic patients, discovered that the non-diabetic obese patients developed a similar resistance due to impairment of glucose tolerance in fasting.

It can thus be seen that the brain is able to adapt quite efficiently to the glucose deprivation of fasting. Evidently, the mild anorexia, euphoria, irritability and childlike behavioral patterns discussed in Chapter 2 are all caused partly by the brain's adaptation to ketosis. If personality changes become pronounced, if there is increased lethargy and depressive behavior, this would clearly indicate the beginning of oxygen deprivation and the need to terminate the fast.

Bibliography

Cheifetz, Philip N.—Uric Acid Excretion and Ketosis in Fasting (*Metabolism, 14,* 1965)

Drenick, Ernst J. et al.—Resistance to Symptomatic Insulin Reactions after Fasting (*J. Clin. Invest., 51,* October 1972)

Foster, Daniel W.—Studies in the Ketosis of Fasting (*J. Clin. Invest., 46,* August 1967)

Genuth, Saul M.—Effects of Prolonged Fasting on Insulin Secretion (*Diabetes, 15,* November 1966)

Smith, Arnold et al.—Induction of Brain D (-) B-Hydroxybutyrate Dehydrogenase Activity by Fasting (*Science, 63,* January 3, 1964)

CHAPTER 5

CONDUCTING A FAST

Having discussed the metabolic changes
which occur during fasting, we must now examine
the best methods of actually conducting a fast.
Given the indications, we believe that fasting is po-
tentially a very beneficial form of therapy. While it
is not without its dangers, these may be circum-
vented by the supplementation of those vitamins
and minerals which are most rapidly lost. It is very
important to remember that the course of the fast
is partially determined by factors such as motivation and mental attitude and that a correct preparation for the fast is absolutely vital.

Preparing for a Fast

It is unwise to consider taking a long fast for the
first time without prior clinical consultation and
without the supervision of a person experienced in
fasting. Before commencing the fast, the system
should be prepared with easily digested foods.
Opinions vary about the type of food advisable, al-

though all agree it should be low calorie and that the meals should not be large. Before long-term fasts, hospitalized patients are often fed low-calorie diets for up to 10 days before a fast. Length of pre-fast preparation would of course depend on the intended length of the fast. A short fast would need little preparation.

Short-Term Fasting

Authorities agree that no definite results can be observed from a fast that lasts only a matter of hours or perhaps the course of a day, but for exceptionally busy persons who have no opportunity to take a long fast or do not feel able to tolerate one, the therapeutic benefit of a short-term or partial fast lies in the brief period of rest which it gives to the organs of digestion. This is a particular advantage when city living gives rise to digestive problems or constipation.

A partial fast might consist in the consumption of one specific food such as fresh juicy fruit or citrus juices or milk products only. A person who is too busy for even this type of fast might consider the possibility of going without one meal. Breakfast would be the easiest meal for most people to skip, since breakfast is usually eaten before any energy has been expended. A 24-hour fast needs very little preparation and could conceivably be taken at a time when optimal relaxation (another prerequisite for a successful fast) is possible. Some nutritionists recommend a weekly 24-hour fast to rest the alimentary tract and cleanse the system.

After a short-term fast such as this, solid food, so long as it is light and easy to digest, can be taken immediately without ill effect. However, no heavy, rich food should be consumed for at least a day.

A fast which is intended to last for anything longer than three days should be carefully prepared for. Begin with a short-term fast and gradually work up to longer periods of fasting. It is, however, inadvisable to attempt to set the exact length of an extended fast in advance, in case any complications occur. Rely on the information of your own body to tell you, before dangerous symptoms set in, just when a fast should be terminated, as well as when it would be beneficial to take a fast. Hopefully, as the body gains in health, this kind of awareness will increase.

Before the fast, the diet should be gradually changed to a low-calorie one. All highly acid-forming foods such as meats, fish and highly seasoned food should be avoided. Fresh fruits and vegetables are excellent, as they also have a purgative effect on the bowels. Also, gradually cut down the amount of food eaten at each meal.

Early fasting experts debated the necessity of taking an enema, laxative or diuretic before fasting. Arnold Ehret, for example, insisted on the absolute necessity of both enemas and laxatives not only before the fast but during its course. Most authorities today regard this treatment with suspicion. On the whole the taking of enemas is considered to be dangerous. Diuretics are definitely considered detrimental, since urinary excretion of electrolytes and water is always excessive except where supplements are given. Laxatives, on the other hand, tend to inhibit excretory function in that they are generally dependency-forming. If you are constipated before the fast, the preferable remedy is fruit juice, particularly prune juice.

The role of vitamin and mineral supplements will be discussed shortly, but for the moment it is sufficient to say that great care must be taken to avoid dehydration, for which the human body has a very low tolerance. Water is needed in large quantities to carry out every function of the body. In this context, the giving of diuretics is extremely harmful although, according to Rooth and Carlstrom, they are frequently given to the obese in fasting. Acidosis already causes abnormal water loss and, if diuretics are given at the beginning of a fast, electrolyte excretion becomes extreme enough to cause death. Water then should be taken regularly during the fast, even if no supplements are taken. The early fasting experts typically advised prospective fasters to drink large amounts of water every hour. However, the best time to drink water is when you yourself are thirsty or, if in doubt, at normal mealtimes.

Another frequent occurrence during fasting is a drop in body temperature owing to postural hypotension, in which case a warm atmosphere is necessary. Extremes of either heat or cold are dangerous. The water drunk should not be refrigerated or even very cold in hot weather. Cold also interferes with elimination so the faster should keep as warm as possible. And even those persons whose metabolism is such that fasting makes them energetic, also require rest. Hard physical labor should be avoided and, if any giddiness or exhaustion occurs, rest immediately. Even important mental labor should be postponed.

It is inadvisable to fast when in a state of anxiety. Stimulants such as drugs, coffee or tea should also be avoided.

More Dangers of Fasting

Some of the dangers of fasting are associated with excessive urinary excretion of water and soluble electrolyte ions, particularly potassium due to acidosis. Although this may have a weakening effect and lead to complications, the effects of hyperdiuresis can be remedied with supplementary minerals. Other dangers spring directly from lack of caution exercised in refeeding. This, too, can be remedied. The most serious criticism of fasting concerns the actual tissue loss. Yet others find negative indications for fasting in the fall of blood pressure, impaired hepatic and renal function during fasting and in side effects such as dizziness, headache and anorexia.

Several deaths have been reported from fasting. Munro and Duncan list the death of one diabetic patient from an apparent lactic acidosis, another suffering from nephritis from renal failure, and several patients from heart failure due to inappropriate fasting. Duncan, Duncan and Schless, University of Pennsylvania researchers, report that atrial flutter developed in three patients during a prolonged fast. However, the researchers add that this condition was affected by the patients' taking too much exercise. They also comment that, in their opinion, fasting is beneficial in certain cases of impaired heart function such as hypertension.

Benoit and his colleagues express concern over the changes in lean body tissue during fasting. In the opinion of this group, the weight losses occurring during fasting were out of proportion to the loss of adipose tissue. They set out to prove that fasting tissue loss contained a dangerous amount of lean flesh. They compared the results of fasting with those of feeding on a ketogenic (i.e., low calorie, high fat) diet which they considered to be of superior effectiveness in the treatment of obesity.

One patient in this study was given first a mixed diet, then a ketogenic diet and then also fasted. Neither of the weight losses from the two diets could compare to the loss from fasting. However, when the weight losses in the group of patients was assessed, it was discovered that of the 9.6-kilogram mean weight loss in fasting patients, 6.2 kgs. was of lean body weight and 3.4 kgs. of body fat. The ketogenic dieters had lost a mean of 6.4 kgs. of body fat with only 0.2 kgs. loss of lean tissue. These findings prompted the researchers to conclude that fasting should not be recommended for the treatment of obesity.

Runcie and Thomson do not agree with these findings, considering fasting both beneficial and effective, despite certain drawbacks such as hyperuricaemia and postural hypotension, which they believe springs from renal excretion of sodium and potassium. They also report on possible complications effecting bowel motility and hypokalaemia which they corrected with glucose tests for carbohydrate intolerance. They concluded that, so long as precautions were taken and protein reserves guarded, the fast would in most cases be beneficial. Fasting would only be dangerous when subjects suffered from liver dysfunction.

Nutritional Supplements

Extensive research leads us to the conclusion that, in most cases of long-term fasting, supplements should be given. The problems which arise with fasting such as impaired glucose tolerance, high levels of mineral excretion, especially of potassium and sodium, and vitamin depletion can easily be reversed by feeding fasting patients with appropriate amounts of supplementary minerals and vitamins or of glucose. The preferred supplement would probably vary according to the metabolism of individual patients.

Potassium depletion is the most striking of the mineral losses. It is also probably the mineral which is most needed because of its reaction with carbohydrate tolerance. In one study in which 14 mEq daily of potassium was given to fasting patients, the glucose tolerance of all patients significantly improved, as did insulin response. The authors of this study believe that fasting potassium deficiency is what leads to glucose intolerance, because insufficient potassium ions are available for enzymatic synthesis of carbohydrates. They also suggest that potassium may be needed to help release insulin from the pancreas. Other researchers consider the addition of small quantities of glucose more practical, both for the conservation of potassium and for other electrolytes and minerals too. Consolazio and colleagues report that ingestion of 100 grams of carbohydrate by a fasting patient reduced both protein and water losses and spared nitrogen from conversion of protein into energy. Glucose supplementation also reduced vitamin excretion and was elsewhere found to have a good effect on sodium loss. Although many vitamins are excreted, it seems that the most research has been done on the effects of Vitamin B excretion. Thiamine, however, is apparently the vitamin most easily lost. For this reason, some researchers recommend the addition of multivitamins for all fasting patients.

Refeeding

Hendrikx and DeMoor re-fed their subjects with glucose for three consecutive days between fasts and before breaking the fast completely. They found that urine volume dropped and remained low even after glucose was given. The potassium of the blood also dropped to a low level and bicarbonate concentration increased. There was also a decrease of serum protein and hemoglobin and hematocrit levels.

Hendrikx and DeMoor then broke the fasts of their subjects with a low calorie (600 calories) diet of protein and carbohydrates which also contained 3000 milligrams of sodium. Immediately, urine volume started to go down and body weight to increase. With the reduction of the sodium, however, the weight gained stabilized. Hendrikx and Moor agree with other researchers that a diet high in fat and low in carbohydrates will in fact induce loss of weight. They attribute the weight loss on a ketogenic diet to water losses.

How to Break a Fast

It is the period directly following a fast which may prove most critical. After fasting, the patient is necessarily in a vulnerable condition, and refeeding should not be allowed to cause any shock to the system, which will take about as much time to regain its digestive and assimilative powers as was spent fasting. It is very dangerous to break a fast on solid food, as the food may decay in the intestinal tract, since the body cannot digest it at this stage of refeeding. If this occurs in the small intestine it will cause, at the very least, great pain. If the peristaltic action of the small intestine fails, the food will become impacted and death may even result. Earlier fasting experts warned adherents of the dangers of breaking fasts incorrectly. It is particularly foolish to attempt to break the fast on heavy protein. Ehret cited lists of deaths from refeeding with such simple foods as potatoes!

The first food taken then, should be liquid. Fruit juices, vegetable juices, milk, or broths made from meat or vegetables all have their advocates. Experience in this matter will teach you what is best but, until then, we would advise that raw fruit juices are the most easily digested. Orange juice made from fresh squeezed oranges can be recommended for those not allergic to it.

At first just a small amount of juice, perhaps half a glass, should be taken. For the first day, frequent small amounts taken regularly are advised by the greatest number of experts. For instance, half a glass of juice can be taken every hour. If, however, you feel unable to drink this amount, it is better to follow your instinct. On the second day, the same juice should be taken, perhaps less frequently or in larger amounts. At no time should each juice meal exceed a pint of liquid. The juice should be sipped slowly and not swallowed immediately, in order to stimulate salivation, and the best temperature is room temperature.

Depending on how long the fast lasted, the juice diet can last up to 6 days. A fast not exceeding 3 days can be followed by a one-day juice diet, even though normal digestion may still be possible. A fast of from 4 to 8 days should be followed by a 2-day juice diet; a fast of from 9 to 15 days probably requires an adjustment period of 3 days. If you fasted for 16 to 24 days it will probably be necessary to take only juice for 4 days and, if the fast was between 25 and 35 days, a 5-day diet of juice should follow. Longer periods will perhaps require 6 days of juice meals. Again, these figures are approximate and will be adjusted to individual requirements once these are recognized.

After the juice diet, the first proper meal should be small and very easy to digest, possibly consisting of steamed and cooked vegetables and fruit. Gradually, the body can return to its normal diet. It should be stressed that now, more than ever, good nutrition habits should be fostered and unsuitable foods avoided.

Living After the Fast

Regular fasts might be a favorable way of maintaining health under ideal circumstances, if only organically grown, unprocessed foods were consumed and adequate rest, exercise and sunlight were available. However, even those of us who are conscious of the vital part that good nutrition plays in our lives are affected by the worst manifestations of urban-industrial civilization.

Nutritionists and other scientists are very fond of quoting statistics about so-called primitive people such as the Hunza who live ideal agrarian existences, are semi-vegetarian, and live extended lives of classic good health in which the degenerative diseases which plague us in the civilized West are almost unknown. Such people need no theoretic knowledge of nutrition, physiology or biochemistry, for that matter, in order to understand what they need to live out their lives and eat the rich-protein foods available to them. The Ethiopians, though poverty-stricken and threatened now by mass death from famine, also are aware which seeds and grains contain the most protein and how they may be utilized.

It is a sad comment on modern civilization with its superior technology and great capacity to research and comprehend the universe that we are for the most part divorced from our bodies and our instincts, of which we are even ashamed to the extent that they exist. However, this need not continue to be so. Paradoxically, it is the scientists who are now exploring ancient knowledge, once logically inexplicable, of the human body and mind and explaining in twentieth-century terms why practices like fasting work. Likewise, modern science is discovering that there is some logical basis for the practice of meditation and its underlying philosophy, and is explaining it with the new technological innovation of biofeedback.

The next part of this book deals with meditation and biofeedback. Some enthusiasts have claimed that meditation can cure the nervous stress that leads to disease. Scientists experimenting with biofeedback training are already discussing the possibility of eliminating the need for some types of orthodox medicine by teaching patients how to cure themselves of their diseases.

We prefer to be more practical and cautious. We do not believe in miracle cures, whether in the realm of orthodox medical practice or against a more antique background like fasting or meditation. We are concerned here with examining a few of the facts, scratching the surface a little and hopefully encouraging our readers to deeper research.

Bibliography

Benoit, R.C. et al.—Changes in Body Composition during Weight Reduction in Obesity: Balance Studies Comparing Effects of Fasting and Ketogenic Diet (*Ann. Internat. Med., 63,* October 1965)

Consolazio, C. Frank et al.—Metabolic Aspects of Calorie Restriction: Nitrogen and Mineral Balances and Vitamin Excretion *(Amer. J. Clin. Nutr., 21,* 8, 1968)

Drenick, Ernst J. and Blahd, William H.—Potassium Supplements during Fasting for Obesity (*Nutr. Rev., 21,* July 1970)

Duncan, G.G. et al.—Contraindications and Therapeutic Results of Fasting in Obese Patients (*Ann. N.Y. Acad. Sci., 131,* October 1965)

Haro, Expedito N. et al.—Fasting in Obesity (*Arch. Internat. Med., 117,* February 1966)

Hendrikx, A. and De Moor, P.—Metabolic Changes in Obese Patients during Fasting and Refeeding (*Acta Med. Belg., 24,* 1964)

Kryzwicki, H.J. et al.—Water and Sodium Retention in the Fasted and Refed Human (*Am. J. Clin. Nutr., 21,* 8, 1968)

Munro, J.F. and Duncan, J.P.—Fasting in the Treatment of Obesity *(Practitioner, 208,* April 1972)

Rooth, G. and Carlstrom, S.—Theraupeutic Fasting (*Acta Med. Scand., 187,* June 1970)

Rooth, G. et al.—Plasma Tocopherol Levels in Therapeutic Starvation (*Internat. J. Vitamin Nutr. Resch., 41,* May 1971)

Runcie, J. and Thomson, T.J.—Prolonged Starvation: A Dangerous Procedure? (*Brit. Med. J., 3,* 1970)

PART II

Meditation and Biofeedback

Chapter 6

MIND OVER MATTER: BIOFEEDBACK

The history of science is filled with instances where ancient, non-scientific practices have been proved not only to be effective but to have a sound scientific basis, and where new scientific ideas have been validated despite hostility from the majority of the professional scientific community.

In the first category can be included the varieties of meditation practices used by many Eastern and some Western religions which, while primarily a road to spiritual knowledge, are, as their modern practitioners claim, of great benefit to both physical and mental health and well-being. The claims of many of the better-known systems of meditation at least have been to some measure borne out in the course of scientifically controlled experimentation, as well as of observation and experience.

In the second category is biofeedback, a technique which teaches people to be aware of the inner workings of their bodies through the use of machinery which has a growing number of adherents and has become the subject of research among scientists of various disciplines, from medical specialists and biologists to engineers, biochemists and sociologists. It has truly revolutionized many previous beliefs about the nature of nerve functioning, but it was also initially the subject of much hostility. Even the earlier research into brain function such as the work done on brain waves by pioneer U.S. researcher Neal E. Miller was considered of such dubious interest that he found it difficult to persuade students to work with him on his projects. Biofeedback enthusiasts now go so far as to claim that their discipline is a way of eradicating all need for conventional medicine, by teaching people to gain complete control over bodily functions. However, this is pure nonsense. It is, moreover, considered by some people to be a means of reaching, in a matter of hours, that state of inner awareness and peace, spiritual and mental, which the practitioners of yoga, Zen and other forms of meditation reach only after many disciplined years.

Biofeedback suggests that information about our inner states is being relayed to us in the same way that information about our surroundings is fed back to us by our senses so that we can learn more about the environment and how to regulate our behavior in reaction to it. The sort of information gained by biofeedback concerns the structural activity of the heart, brain, various other organs, blood circulation, respiration; information, in short, which is normally inaccessible. Biofeedback techniques and training are part of a technological system. Paradoxically, biofeedback has also become a means by which the claims of ancient meditation and religious practices have been tested and proved and given a somewhat different emphasis.

Before any discussion of biofeedback is possible, however, we must first talk a little about the function of the nervous system and the brain and some of the research which biofeedback has affected and which it is affected by.

The Nervous System

There are two nervous systems of the body, the functions of which are quite distinct. The first, the central nervous system, sometimes called the somatic nervous system, controls the entire skeleton, all the muscles and joints of the limbs and all their movements, by means of the 31 pairs of nerves which are connected to the central nervous system where it is enclosed by the spinal cord. The central nervous system also includes the brain and the 12 pairs of nerves which control its impulses.

The other nervous system, the autonomic nervous system, runs along the spinal cord and controls the functioning of the body within the skeletal frame; the internal organs such as the heart, liver, pancreas, stomach; glands such as the sweat and the salivary glands; the respiratory and circulatory systems and the millions of small muscles of those organs, glands and systems, in the cells of the blood vessels, the iris of the eye and so on.

Learning and the Autonomic System

The idea that it is possible to control at will the functioning of what were considered to be involuntary impulses in the same way as, say, the limbs can be controlled, although not a new idea to anyone who has studied the writings and teachings of the many esoteric religious and mystic practitioners of meditation who had for thousands of years claimed the ability to control their bodies at will, is still not entirely acceptable to those who only have available to them the benefits of our superior biological knowledge.

The first incontrovertible evidence that the autonomic nervous system is capable of learning was given by Dr. Neal E. Miller in his experiments at Rockefeller University, New York. Initial experiments used rats whose skeletal muscles had been paralyzed with the drug, curare. This was necessary in order to prove that the learning process did go on in the autonomic nervous system and was set up by visceral responses and that it was not by some skeletal impulse that the animals were able to control their heart rate, blood pressure and other responses. For instance, it is said that the yogic meditator controls his (or her) breathing through expansion of the rib cage. Miller was in fact successful in training first rats and then other animals, including dogs, to manipulate various "involuntary" nervous functions, and to do this despite the difficulty of instituting the usual series of rewards and punishments through which animals are encouraged to learn skills. As the paralyzed rats were unable to eat, drink or breathe (they had to be fed air by means of an artificial respirator machine), the method of reward used was a pleasurable electrical stimulation of the brain. Not only were the rats able to learn to manipulate and control various responses, they were able to retain the learning processes and repeat them on separate occasions.

Miller's initial experiments opened up the way for future work on autonomic learning and to experimentation with the machinery associated with biofeedback training. With his colleague Carmona,

Miller trained rats to raise or lower the voltage of their brain waves as proved by the electroencephalograph.

Brain Waves

Recent neurological research began with the discovery of the existence of brain waves in 1924 by German physicist Hans Berger, who, believing that the brain stored energy in the form of electricity which in turn dominated various states of consciousness, set about proving his theories, in spite of apparent hostility from fellow scientists. After many years of research, his first success came when the galvanometer attached to his crude electrical impulse-recording device recorded a definite response from the brain of the young mental patient whom Berger was using as a subject. Berger was able to establish the existence of two types of brain wave which he named alpha and beta respectively. The alpha waves were recorded when the subject was in a state of relaxation or passivity, while the beta waves were connected with states of concentrated activity. Berger's work was never finished. He ran into trouble with the Nazis when they came into power, was dismissed from his work at the University of Jena where he had been carrying out his research, and subsequently killed himself.

The machine now used to record brain waves is the electroencephalograph or EEG machine. Like Berger's early machine, it employs several electrodes which are attached to the scalp of the subject and an amplifier which transmits the brain's activity and relays the impulses to a row of pens which record the patterns made by the different brain waves onto a roll of paper. Through the use of this device, we now know of the existence of four types of brain waves, although the existence of more is, of course, always a possibility. Additional ones called alpha and beta waves which Berger discovered are already known, besides the theta and delta. The brain wave of highest frequency, which is recorded at 14 cycles a second, is beta, associated with the alert state of mind, with concentration, study and much of the day's normal activity.

The rhythms of the different brain waves are quite distinct. Beta is rapid, somewhat jerky; alpha is smooth and slower than beta; while theta and delta waves are respectively slower than alpha. Alpha waves have a frequency scale of between 8 and 13 cycles a second, and the alpha state is usually considered to be one of relaxation. Theta waves, which record a frequency of 4 to 7 cycles a second, are most commonly associated with the time just before the onset of sleep but are also connected with creative states, hallucination and sometimes anxiety. Delta is the lowest recorded brain wave with a frequency rate of between one half and six cycles a second and it is not generally recorded outside the sleeping state.

It is believed that the rhythms of the brain waves are the result of electrochemical impulses occurring in the cells of the brain when they are sending out information to various parts of the body. Generally speaking, brain rhythms are in flux, the frequency level changing as the brain goes from alpha into beta and back again. Also, the two halves of the brain often record different waves at the same time; for example, the left half may be in alpha when the right hemisphere is in beta.

Biofeedback and the Brain

By using the various instruments of biofeedback —the electroencephalograph which records brain waves, the electromyograph which charts muscular tension—the subject first becomes aware of what is going on within his or her body and then, with expert guidance, learns how some of those functions can be mentally controlled. In this way, it may be possible for improvements in health to result; for example, the patient may be able to learn how to reduce the level of blood pressure when it is too high. Biofeedback training has, of course, reached fad proportions in some areas and like many another craze, extravagant claims have been made for it, as a potential cure for every imaginable ill, both physical and mental, as well as a way of instantly reaching states of almost religious experience.

However, biofeedback as a science and as a technique for learning self-awareness and for improving health is very much in its infancy, although many excellent results have been obtained. A knowledge of the functions of the body and brain which can be affected by biofeedback training is hardly much less recent.

It was in 1958 that Joseph Kamiya, then working at the University of Chicago where he was doing research into sleep patterns, had the idea that it might be possible to teach a subject to be aware of his or her changing brain rhythms. To see if there was any foundation for this idea, Kamiya attached the electrodes of an EEG machine to the head of a subject who was isolated in a darkened room. The subject's task was to say, when he heard a bell ring, if he thought he was in the alpha state of consciousness or another state. After his guess he would be told whether he had given the correct answer or not. On the first day of the experiments, the subject guessed correctly about half the time, but as the week progressed, he made more and more correct guesses until by the fourth day he was fully aware of when he was in the alpha state and when he was not. The same experience proved true of eleven other subjects.

Not only were the subjects able to learn when they were in the alpha state, they were also able to learn how to enter that state and remain in it at will. Kamiya was able to shorten the time it took his subjects to exercise control over their alpha states, using the method of biofeedback. Now, when the EEG machinery registered alpha wave formation, another device informed the subject of the fact by a special tone which in many cases, at least under laboratory conditions, accelerated learning ability. Good subjects could learn to control their brain waves within a few hours.

Since Kamiya's initial experiments, it has been found possible to control the other types of brain waves and the technique of biofeedback training has become somewhat more sophisticated. Its uses have been extended and its possibilities begin to seem endless. In the field of brain research, Dr. Robert Orstein of the Langley-Porter Neuropsychiatric Institute was recently researching the possibilities of controlling the separate processes of either the left or right hemisphere of the brain.

The Two Sides of the Brain

That the two hemispheres of the brain have different functions had been known or at any rate hypothesized for many years. Recent research, such as that undertaken by Joseph Borgen, gave evidence that the left and right hemispheres not only have different functions but can be successfully separated from each other.

Hippocrates recognized that the brain had a dual function. A. I. Wigan in 1844 declared that each cerebrum could function as if it were one complete brain. The first known hemispherectomy was performed in 1888 by Goltz, who removed the entire left hemisphere of the brain from a dog and noted that its behavior was little altered by its loss. Removal of the left or right hemisphere of the brain from human subjects began, as a treatment for epilepsy, in 1950, and again it was noted that neither behavior nor intelligence was drastically altered.

Wigan was of the opinion that the possession of two cerebral hemispheres implied the existence of two minds. Split brain surgery substantially proved this. Initial split brain surgery was conducted in 1953 by Myers and Sperry with subsequent work by Gazzaniga and Young in 1967 and Bogen, Sperry and Vogel in 1969 and 1970. In the first experiments, on cats, the connecting nerve tissue between the left and right cerebral hemisphere (called the *corpus callosum*) was cut. In the initial experiment, Myers and Sperry also severed the connection between the optic nerves so that each eye functioned separately. In this way, the animal was taught to recognize a problem with one eye. Once this eye had been trained, it was found that the process had to be repeated over again for the second eye and the other half of the brain. In later experiments using monkeys, the two parts of the brain could be conditioned to carry out different activities which were sometimes contradictory. It was revealed in the experiments using human subjects suffering from epilepsy that the left side of the brain controlled the motor responses of the right side of the body and vice versa. At first it was thought that no personality change resulted from split brain surgery, but tests revealed that the two halves of the brain do in fact have entirely different capacities, just as Wigan had thought. The left hemisphere is now considered to control the rational, organizing, linear, linguistic function, while the right is associated with the emotional, creative, non-linear, visual approach. Possibly further research will reveal that we possess yet other levels of consciousness and that they will be found to operate within either the left or right hemisphere. In the meanwhile, the duality of the brain opens up all sorts of interesting questions. It can be seen that in the West we have a predilection for the left, the logical-propositional side of the brain, for we consider its function superior to that of the right. Possibly such a predilection is inevitable as a result of our dual consciousness.

Biofeedback and Control

Ornstein, among others, has suggested that as biofeedback reveals more and more about the workings of the brain, we will learn to control completely our moods, emotions and reactions to experience. But the prospect of the scientific control and conditioning of human behavior through the use of drugs, psychosurgery and electrical manipulation of the brain has become more and more frightening in recent years. The possibility that biofeedback techniques could be used for this kind of control should not be ignored. So far at least, biofeedback has been used only in a way which involves the individual's personal control of response. Even so, the question can be asked, is not this type of conditioned response, even when self-induced, somewhat akin to the kind of behavior modification advocated by such psychologists as B.F. Skinner? The problem is indeed one of the central ones of modern Western civilization.

In defense of biofeedback, its exciting possibilities for expanding self-awareness have been suggested as a solution to Western man's alienation from his body. On this matter, it can be asked, for instance, why a machine is necessary in the first place to inform a subject of the state of his or her consciousness as manifested in the patterns of the brain waves. That is, if the alpha state can be seen to manifest itself during periods of relaxation, why should we not be immediately aware of this?

The fact is that most of us are not aware of how we feel at all, a consequence of the sort of society in which we live, dominated by stresses and strains, by considerations of time, money, status, subject to problems of an exceedingly complex nature; a society in which it is almost impossible to relax. It is beginning to be generally recognized that many people are "out of touch" with their feelings, an abnormal mental state which once recognized should not be accepted as inevitable.

Perhaps this is one very positive contribution that biofeedback can make. For to get in touch with the inner workings of one's psyche requires far more time and discipline than many Americans are able to put in after an exhausting day. For many the process of meditation is incomprehensible and, for many others, the nearest they can come to satori is a few minutes spent on yoga exercises every week or so, rather in the way that, knowing something of nutrition, a person might balance a normally unhealthy diet by occasionally eating an organic meal in a health food restaurant. The problem is not so much the lack of time but an attitude of mind which tends to predominate in this culture and which dictates that it is more important to save time than to conserve one's health and that anything that does not give immediate results is a waste of time.

Thus the value of biofeedback. Apart from the very definite contribution it has to make to health, it can, merely as an experimental device, open people to the possibilities of true relaxation, of truly becoming aware of not only the tissues, bones and blood which make up their bodies, but also what is happening in their minds. As Eleanor Criswell of Sonoma State College in California states, biofeedback can be extremely helpful even if the machinery used is faulty, simply because it is quietly relaxing to the person using it. Criswell also makes the point that the gadgetry involved in biofeedback makes it highly sympathetic to the American character. Rather paradoxically, that gadgetry may be one product of the very technology that has made our lives so complex, which will lead us to a reconsideration of the quality of life. However, Criswell appears to believe wholeheartedly in the beneficial effects to be derived from biofeedback training, a belief not shared by all specialists.

Effects of Alpha Waves

One reason why a subject may not recognize the alpha state is that this state of consciousness does not manifest itself in the same way to everyone. For a majority of people perhaps, the alpha state is one of calm relaxation. For some, it is merely a brain-wave frequency of between 8 and 13 cycles per second. One yogi said that he felt "nothing" when he went into alpha. For a few people, alpha is an unpleasant experience associated with anxiety. For others, it is related to lack of concentration. One scientist discovered in tests on students who did badly at school for no apparent reason, that these same students had unusually high levels of alpha wave activity. Some people experience feelings during alpha that others have in theta.

Theta, too, has varying effects on people. Herschel Toomin, an engineer involved in a theta feedback experiment in which 26 people learned to control their theta waves, explains that while half the people experienced the theta state as a creative one, a few had feelings of anxiety and frustration. Swami Rama finds theta to be an anxious, tense state. More research needs to be done into brain function to understand whether creativity is linked with anxiety.

Health Without Medicine?

Biofeedback training as an addition to other forms of preventive medicine is neither a far-fetched idea nor, in all probability, very far away from being a reality. Already a number of very useful, very promising results have been achieved and a great deal of research is being conducted in the treatment of various conditions. The argument behind biofeedback training is that a patient can learn to eradicate the source of the health problem by locating the organ or part of the body where the problem arises and making it behave in such a way that improve-

ment is effected. The use of EEG biofeedback as a
diagnostic tool seems promising. Work is being done
in this area by Thomas Mulholland in Boston, who
is investigating biofeedback as a means to discovering brain disease and malfunction. Joseph Kamiya
believes that neurotics could use biofeedback to
learn to behave in a more healthy way. Biofeedback
could possibly take the place of tranquilizing drugs.
Erik Peper is experimenting with alpha feedback as
a possible future substitute for anaesthesia to control pain and eventually overcome it. Others are conducting research into the possibility of using biofeedback to produce states pleasurable enough to
replace drugs or alcohol and to help patients overcome these addictions. Very few parts of the body
have not been monitored to see if control is possible
in yet other areas.

One condition which is the subject of major concern, namely hypertension, has responded well to
biofeedback experiments. As we mentioned in
Chapter 4, drug therapy has not proved very successful in the treatment of hypertensive diseases.
Although weight reduction and regular exercise
have been useful in reducing dangerous levels of
blood pressure when obesity is the main cause,
where the condition is advanced, these methods may
be insufficient. It is here that biofeedback training
in conjunction with a revised life style has been
proved effective. Noteworthy among researchers in
this area are David Shapiro of the Harvard Medical
School, Jasper Brehner of the University of Ten-
nessee, Herbert Benson at Harvard and Aimee
Christy and John Vitale of the San Francisco Veterans Hospital. In their studies, patients who were
taught with the aid of light and sound feedback "to
listen" to their blood pressure, were able, in the ma-

jority of cases, to control their blood pressure levels in the laboratory. Benson reported success in 5 out of 7 cases. The next step is for hypertensives to be trained to control their blood pressure outside the laboratory without the benefit of feedback from machines. A simple portable machine has been suggested, whereby the patient could test the level of the blood pressure at regular intervals. But to listen to the rhythms of one's own blood is not a concept which comes easily to Westerners!

Some success in training patients to control their irregular heartbeats outside the laboratory and in the home environment has been reported. Bernard T. Engel, Theodore Weiss and K. Melmon of Baltimore City Hospital report that of 8 patients, 3 were able to achieve spontaneous cardiac control after lengthy laboratory training.

Other researchers have been speaking hypothetically yet optimistically of the eventual use of EMG biofeedback training to cure cancer by forcing the body to absorb tumorous growths. Kamiya and Mulholland of the Langley-Porter Neurological Institute are confident that the effects of brain damage and all kinds of mental and behavioral disorders can be unlearned. Some of the most successful results have been achieved with stress-related disorders. Paul Grim stresses the importance of respiration biofeedback in combating anxiety and tension, suggesting that it is breath control which is most important in relaxation. University of Colorado biofeedback researchers Johann Stoyva and Thomas Budzynski differ from Grim in believing that muscular tension should first be eradicated in therapy. Accordingly, they teach subjects to control the frontalis muscle of the forehead with the use of the EMG machine. They feel that anxiety could disappear as a result of deep relaxation. By controlling alpha levels, anxious or depressed patients have been able to eradicate or reduce their intake of tranquilizing drugs. The sort of relaxation that can help cure anxiety symptoms also can be taught with the use of EMG and EEG feedback in a matter of a few hours.

Another stress-related condition that has been dealt with very successfully with biofeedback training is migraine. Much work in this area was done at the Menninger Foundation of Topeka, Kansas, conducted by Elmer Green, his wife, Alyce, and his colleagues. In many cases, it was discovered, migraine and tension headaches will disappear when the warmth of the hand is increased and that of the forehead decreased, though no reason has as yet been established. Therefore, patients are taught to control their blood flow in such a way as to ensure the warm hands, cool forehead effect. One of Green's patients, a migraine sufferer for many years, learned to control her headaches in this way within a period of two weeks and subsequently reported after several years that she had not suffered from another migraine headache in all that time.

In biofeedback, as in meditation, the importance of expert instruction must be emphasized. Attempts to control one's internal impulses without a proper understanding of the processes at work can be disastrous. Nonetheless, this sort of control goes on, subconsciously perhaps, all the time. Many psychosomatic diseases are caused by subconscious control of digestive functions, for instance, or of blood circulation. Green and his colleague Sargent discovered in the course of their migraine researches at the Menninger Foundation that certain patients were able to produce migraine headaches at will, when, for example, they felt threatened in some way.

Mind Over Matter

Is there anything so very surprising about our ability to control our own inner impulses? The term "psychosomatic" has been common parlance for several years, and various disorders are frequently alluded to as emotional in origin. "Mind over matter" is another common expression. The use of the placebo, a sugar-coated pill made to look like an actual drug which it replaces, is common in medical research. Often, out of simple faith in the effects of the drug, a patient will have symptoms immediately alleviated on swallowing the placebo. This does not mean that the illness is "psychosomatic" in origin; it simply signifies that we have far more control over our nervous systems than we are aware, more control than many doctors, physiologists or psychiatrists would, for many years, have admitted.

For those to whom the rational, practical aspects of life are paramount, the mystic experience is alien to an understanding of the world. However, it has been pointed out that the idea of an underlying harmony in nature is shared not only by Eastern religions and Western mystics, but also by many Western scientists. Einstein's view of reality was similar to that of many mystics.

What is particularly important to understand about the use of both meditation techniques and biofeedback training in the improvement of health is that they involve a real knowledge of the self.

In addition, biofeedback training involves a galaxy of complex electrical equipment. Although several machines are on the market, of both the

EEG and EMG varieties, and even portable, light-weight versions are being researched and produced, we do not advise the reader to invest in one for home use unless he or she possesses a great deal of skilled knowledge. Their use implies the possession of not only engineering knowhow but also a thorough knowledge of neurophysiological function. If you are interested in finding out more about biofeedback, find out if any programs of research into biofeedback are being carried out at local universities and colleges and, if there are, investigate the possibility of offering yourself as a subject.

Bibliography

Albino, R. and Burnand, G.—Conditioning of the Alpha Rhythm in Man (*J. Exp. Psych.*, 67, 1964)

Anderson, S.—Warm Hands Mean a Cool Quiet Head (*Midway, Magazine of the Topeka-Capital Journal*, August 15, 1971)

Barber, T.—Biofeedback and Self-Control (Chicago: Aldine-Atherton, 1970)

Barratt, P. and Herd, J.—Subliminal Conditioning of Alpha Rhythm (*Austral. J. Psych.*, 16, 1964)

Basmajian, J.—Muscles Alive: Their Functions Revealed by Electromyography (Baltimore: Williams and Wilkins, 1967)

Bay, E.—Aphasia an Intelligence (*Internat. J. Neurol.*, 4, 1964)

Beatty, J.—Effects of Initial Alpha Wave Abundance and Operant Training Procedures on Occipital Alpha and Beta Wave Activity (*Psychosom. Sci.*, 23, 1971)

Bell, E. and Karnosh, E.J.—Cerebral Hemispherectomy: Report of a Case Ten Years After Operation (*J. Neurosurgery*, 6, 1949)

Benson, H. et al.—Decreased Systolic Blood Pressure Through Operant Conditioning Techniques in Patients with Essential Hypertension (*Science, 173*, 1971)

Birk, L. et al.—Operant Electrodermal Conditioning Under Partial Curarization (*J. Comp. Physiol. Psych., 32,* 1966)

Bogen, J.E.—The Other Side of the Brain: An Appositional Mind *(Bull. L.A. Neurol. Soc., 34,* 1969)

Bogen, J.E. and Bogen, C.M.—The Other Side of the Brain: The Corpus Callosum and Creativity (*Bull. L.A. Neurol. Soc., 34,* 1969)

Bogen, J.E. and Gazzaniga, M.S.—Cerebral Commisurotomy in Man: Minor Hemisphere Dominance for Certain Visuospatial Functions (*J. Neurosurgery, 23,* 1965)

Brener, J. and Hothersall, D.—Heartrate Control Under Conditions of Augmented Sensory Feedback (*Psychophysiology, 3,* 1966)

Brown, B.—Recognition of Aspects of Consciousness through Association with EEG Alpha Activity Represented by a Light Signal (*Psychophysiology, 6,* 1970)

Budzynski, T. and Stoyva, J.—Biofeedback Techniques in Behavior Therapy and Autogenic Training (University of Colorado, 1971, unpublished ms.)

Budzynski, T. and Stoyva, J.—An Instrument for Producing Deep Muscle Relaxation by Means of Analog Information Feedback *(J. Appl. Behav. Anal., 2,* 1969)

Chadwick, J. and Mann, W.N.—*The Medical Works of Hippocrates* (Oxford: Blackwell, 1950)

Christy, A. and Vitale, J.—Operant Conditioning of High Blood Pressure: A Pilot Study (San Francisco Veterans Administration Hospital, 1971, unpublished ms.)

Clemente, C.—Comments on the Brain as an Effective Organ for Studying Conditioned Reflexes (*Conditioned Reflex, 5,* 1970)

Darley, F.L. (ed.)—*Brain Mechanisms Underlying Speech and Language* (New York: Grune and Stratton, 1966)

Darrow, C. and Gullickson, G.—The Role of Brain Waves in Learning and Other Integrative Functions (*Recent Advances in Biological Psychiatry, 10,* 1968)

Deikman, A.—Implications of Experimentally Induced Meditative Contemplation (*J. Nerv. & Mental Disease, 142,* 1966)

Deikman, A.—Bimodal Consciousness (*Arch. Gen. Psychiat., 25,* 1971)

DiCara, L.—Learning in the Autonomic Nervous System (*Scientific American, 222,* 1970)

DiCara, L. and Miller, N.—Instrumental Learning of Systolic Blood Pressure Responses by Curarized Rats: Disassociation of Cardiac and Vascular Changes (*Psychosom. Med., 30,* 1968)

Engel, B.T. and Melmon, K.—Operant Conditioning of Heart Rate in Patients with Cardiac Arrhythmias (*Conditional Reflex, 3,* 1968)

Fenton, G. and Scotton, L.—Personality and the Alpha Rhythm (*Br. J. Psychiat., 113,* 1967)

Fenwick, P.B.C.—*The Effects of Eye Movement on Alpha Rhythm* (New York)

Gazzaniga, M.—*The Bisected Brain* (New York: Appleton, 1970)

Gazzaniga, M.S., Bogen, J.E. and Sperry, R.W.—Observations on Visual Perception after Disconnection of the Cerebral Hemispheres in Man (*Brain, 88,* 1965)

Goltz, F.—On the Functions of the Hemispheres, in Von Bonin—*Some Papers in the Cerebral Cortex* (Springfield, Ill.: Charles C. Thomas, 1960)

Green, Elmer E. et al.—Voluntary Control of Internal States: Psychological and Physiological *(J. Transpers. Psych., 5,* 1969)

Grim, P.—Anxiety Change Produced by Self-Induced Muscle Tension and by Relaxation with Respiratory Feedback (*Behav. Therapy, 2,* 1971)

Hare, R. and Quinn, M.—Psychopathy and Autonomic Conditioning *(J. Abnormal Psychology, 77,* 1971)

Hilgard, E.—Altered States of Awareness (*J. Nervous & Mental Disease, 149,* 1969)

Hill, D. and Parr, G.—*Electroencephalography* (New York: Macmillan, 1963)

Isaacson, R.—*Basic Readings on Neuropsychology* (New York: Harper & Row, 1964)

Kamiya, J.—Conscious Control of Brain Waves (*Psychology Today, 1,* 1968)

Kamiya, J.—A Fourth Dimension of Consciousness (*J. Exper. Med. & Surgery, 27,* 1969)

Karlins, Marvin and Andrews, Lewis M.—*Biofeedback* (New York: Warner Paperback Library, 1972)

Kimmel, K.—Instrumental Conditioning of Autonomically Mediated Behavior (*Psychol. Bull., 67,* 1967)

Lang, P.—Autonomic Control or Learning to Play the Internal Organs (*Phychology Today,* October 1970)

London, P.—*Behavioral Control* (New York: Harper & Row, 1969)

Lowinger, P. and Dobie, S.—What Makes the Placebo Work? (*Arch. Gen. Psych., 20,* 1969)

Luce, Gay—*Body Time* (New York: Pantheon, 1971)

Luce, G. and Peper, E.—Biofeedback: Mind over Body, Mind over Mind *(N.Y. Times Magazine,* September 12, 1971)

Mayr, O.—The Origins of Feedback Control *(Scientific American 223,* 1970)

Miller, N.E.—Learning of Visceral and Glandular Responses (*Science,* 1969)

Miller, N.—Psychosomatic Effects of Specific Types of Learning (*Ann. N.Y. Acad. Sci., 159,* 1969)

Myers, R.E. and Sperry, R.W.—Interocular Transfer of a Visual Form Discrimination Habit in Cats after Section of the Optic Chiasma and Corpus Callosum (*Anatomical Record, 115,* 1953)

Olds, J.—The Central Nervous System and the Reinforcement of Behavior (*Am. Psychologist, 24,* 1969)

Parades, E. et al.—A Clinical Study of Alcoholics Using Audiovisual Self-image Feedback (*J. Nervous & Mental Disease,* 1969)

Rosenfeld, J. et al.—Operant Control of Neural Events in Humans (*Science, 165,* 1969)

Sargent, J. et al.—Preliminary Report on the Use of Autogenic Feedback Techniques in the Treatment of Migraine and Tension Headache (Menninger Foundation, 1971, unpublished ms.)

Shapiro, D. et al.—Control of Diastolic Blood Pressure in Man by Feedback and Reinforcement (*Psychophysiology,* 1973)

Shipman, W. et al.—Muscle Tension and Effort at Self Control during Anxiety (*Arch. Gen. Psychiat.*, 23, 1970)

Skinner, B.F.—*Beyond Freedom and Dignity* (New York: Knopf, 1971)

Sperry, R.—A Modified Concept of Consciousness (*Psychol. Revw.*, 76, 1969)

Tani, K. and Yoshii, N.—Efficiency of Verbal Learning During Sleep as Related to EEG Pattern (*Brain Research*, 17, 1970)

Wigan, A.I.—*The Duality of the Mind* (London: Longmans, 1844)

88. BIOFEEDBACK, FASTING & MEDITATION

CHAPTER 7

MEDITATION AND THE HUMAN SYSTEM

Scientists of several disciplines have been eager to find out if the achievement of physiological and mental control by some of the practitioners of meditation can be scientifically explained. Since recent discoveries about brain function and subsequent research into the technique of biofeedback, the claims of the meditators have become easier to understand and to accept. By utilizing the machinery which biofeedback has made familiar, scientists have been able to perceive the physiological and brain wave changes which occur during the course of various meditative practices.

It has been principally the better-known systems of the East which have been tested, yoga and Zen meditation (Zazen). In general, practitioners of these and other systems of meditation dispute biofeedback enthusiasts who claim they can duplicate the achievements of meditation and arrive at the kind of inner awareness and peace, the transcendence of ego, which most meditators have as their goal and reach in a few hours. Some purists do not believe that a similar experience, if produced through biofeedback, would be a genuine one, but for other people biofeedback seems more practical.

Some members of this latter group would be uncomfortable with the esoteric aspects of meditation with its emphasis on nonverbal knowledge, intuition and spiritual values—those functions, that is, of the right side of the brain, which we in the West have to some measure been conditioned to distrust. (However, this distrust is beginning to fade in the light of modern scientific investigation.)

The dispute between meditators and biofeedbackers is not one which we have any inclination to enter in this chapter. What concerns us here are the results achieved through the means of meditation, specifically those aspects which affect the health of the individual meditator. It is also not within the scope of this book to examine in any detail the philosophy of any of the meditation practices which we shall discuss, fascinating as the subject is. This does not imply that we consider the practical aspects of meditation to be more important than the philosophical-religious systems which underlie them or that we discount the methods used in favor of the scientific approach of biofeedback. This is far from the case. However, as this book is most concerned with meditation as a remedy for common health problems, it is those more practical aspects which we have chosen to present. Therefore, it will be noted, our bibliography to this chapter lists mostly literature dealing with scientific research.

Yoga

Advanced practitioners of the various disciplines

of yoga claim extraordinary capacities of physiological control such as the ability to control blood
temperature to endure extreme cold, to fast for ex-
ceptional lengths of time, and to hold the breath for
extended periods. One of the earliest objective investigations of such claims was undertaken by
Therese Bosse, a French cardiologist in India in
1935. She conducted her tests, for which she used a
small portable electrocardiograph, on several yogis
who claimed that they could stop their hearts from
beating. One of her tests proved that one man could
indeed stop his heart. The exact technique by
which he attained this was probably an exercise
known as Valsava in which the breath is held and
the muscles of the thorax contracted while the meditator pushes his concentration downward.

Later researchers do not altogether bear out
Bosse's findings. Physiologists M.A. Wenger of
U.C.L.A., B.K. Bagchi of the University of Michi-
gan Medical School and B.K. Anand of the All-
India Institute of Medical Sciences in New Delhi
used more elaborate equipment in their 1957 studies on yogis. None of their subjects proved to be
able to stop his heart, and the researchers concluded that when Bosse's subject contracted his thorax
muscles, he somehow blocked the electrical impulses
normally recorded by the electrocardiograph. However, they did find that a great many of the yogis
they tested were able to reduce both heartbeat and
respiration levels.

One particularly impressive feat was recorded in
1956 by a team of psychologists and physicians of
the World Health Organization in conjunction with
the All-India Institute for Mental Health in Bangalore. They were to oversee the experiment, the conditions of which had been set up by the subject

himself, the Yogi Shri S.R. Khrishna Iyengar. The yogi entered a deep pit, was connected by means of wires to the various instruments which would monitor his vital functions such as the heartbeat and respiration and then was buried in the pit. Earth was piled on top of the pit and then it was covered with wooden planks. The researchers were, in fact, fearful for the yogi's life if he was to stay in the pit for the 35 hours which he himself had set as his time limit, so they set a new time limit of nine hours. It was estimated that in a period of nine hours no more than one cubic meter of air would be able to enter the pit through spaces between the crumbs of earth on top of the boards, and that this amount of air was insufficient for survival. After the nine hours of the experiment, the yogi climbed out of the pit. He appeared to be in very much the same state as when he had entered it. In order to survive on his reduced air capacity, the yogi had successfully slowed down his metabolism to reduce his need for oxygen.

A somewhat similar experiment carried out in 1961 in New Delhi by B.K. Anand, G.S. China and Baldeu Singh with the cooperation of the yogi Shri Ramanand Yogi produced similar evidence. In this experiment, the yogi was able to cut down his need for oxygen as well as his need to get rid of carbon dioxide in order to stay alive in an airtight box.

Zen Meditation

The ability to slow down the rate of metabolism is shared by Zen meditators, as has been demonstrated by various studies. Y. Sugi and K. Akatsu tested a number of Zen monks and found that, on average, they were able to reduce their need for oxygen by about 20 percent during meditation.

Tokyo University scientists Akira Kasamatsu and Tomio Hirai investigated both the psychological and physiological aspects of Zen Buddhist meditation, using the electroencephalograph. The experiment involved 48 Zen priests and disciples whose EEG patterns were recorded before, during and after meditation. Here is a brief account of their findings.

After about 50 seconds of meditation, alpha waves appeared. This occurred, the researchers report, whether or not the eyes of the subject were closed. The amplitude of the alpha waves increased and then, as the level of the meditation deepened, the alpha frequency decreased to about 7 or 8 cycles a second. In some subjects, the frequency level slowed down until the meditators were showing theta brain waves. The appearance of these waves was considered by a Zen Master to correlate to the disciple's states of mind in meditation, the final goal of which is to reach a state where the mind is blank, free of attachment to all objects, unconscious of self.

Meditation and Biofeedback

EEG tests performed in India during yogic meditation also reveal a pattern of deepening alpha states. These were carried out by Anand and his colleagues and by N.N. Das and H. Gastaut. In the Das-Gastaut experiment, seven yogis manifested a rapid increase in brain wave frequency after the initial appearance of alpha. However, these waves, some of which registered between 40 and 45 cycles a second, gave way after a few seconds to alpha, after which a slow, smooth descent into theta appeared, as in the case of the Zen meditators. Researchers Gay Luce and Erik Peper report of a Peruvian meditator, Ramon Torres, that his EEG reading, recorded while he was engaged in sticking sharpened spikes through the flesh of his face, was high alpha.

Many researchers believe that once the exact neurophysiological patterns occurring during meditation have been discovered, the teaching of meditation techniques through biofeedback training will be simplified. Johann Stoyva of the University of Colorado believes that a patient might be enabled to learn the blank mind state which Zazen produces within a few hours. Joseph Kamiya is another biofeedback enthusiast who believes that even a subject who had never attempted to meditate before could be quite easily schooled to mimic the results. The general belief among researchers is that those biofeedback subjects able to produce alpha waves easily and to experience the alpha state as a pleasant and relaxing one, can learn to produce EEG correlates of meditation quickly.

Not every researcher agrees however. Among scientists who have made extensive studies of meditation, Robert Wallace feels that, in fact, there is no exact physiological pattern common to all meditative states. In fact they vary greatly sometimes even within the same discipline, as can be seen by comparing the findings above on yogic EEG waves and those common to Zazen. Wallace believes that when attempts are made to control the consciousness by artificial means such as biofeedback, a strain is imposed on the system, an imbalance which results from concentrating on one bodily function. He feels that biofeedback produces not an altered state of consciousness, but an altered state of wakefulness.

Transcendental Meditation

Wallace chose the yoga technique of Transcendental Meditation (TM) for in-depth experiments partly because, like Zen meditation, it encompasses a standardized technique. Yoga practices differ enormously even though their goals are similar. Some yogic meditation is contemplative, some consists of rigorous mental exercises, other varieties use difficult physical exercises. Nearly all yogic meditation entails a great deal of time, much practice and great discipline.

Perhaps it is the relative simplicity of the practice of TM that has won it so many Western disciples. It involves no specific beliefs or life style and, most important, is easily learned in a far shorter period than most forms of meditation. It only requires learning to concentrate on a sound or possibly a thought considered to be suitable, while sitting comfortably, eyes closed. It is taught by instructors personally chosen by TM's founder, Maharishi Mahesh Yogi. TM displays a kind of marriage between Eastern mysticism and Western popular deductive thought and no doubt owes much of its success to this, too. Ex-physicist Maharishi Mahesh Yogi offers in his own writings clear and logically simple explanations of some of the physiological processes that occur during his type of meditation. He emphasizes practical considerations above religious content as, for instance, in his explanation of the use of the mantra, that particular sound or word on which a meditator concentrates at the beginning of the exercise. In some meditation practices, the repetition of the mantra is designed to bring the meditator into union with the universe, as with the yogic "om," or to identify with God, as with the suffix "hoo." Maharishi explains to his disciples that if they concentrate their attention on the proper mantra, they will be enabled to control their breath. The shallower state of breathing which results lowers the amount of carbon dioxide produced in the blood plasma and thus reduces the energy needs of the body. It is this process which produces a state of calm and restful contemplation.

TM Research

The most detailed findings of Wallace and his colleague, Herbert Benson, involved 36 subjects ranging in age from 17 to 41 observed at two separate locations, the University of California at Irvine and the Harvard Medical Unit. Some of the subjects had been meditating for several years, some for only a few months and others for two or three days. However, because the initial training period required to master the technique is short, the difference in experience did not cause the sort of problems that more complicated forms of yoga would. Heart rate, skin resistance, blood temperature and pressure, and EEG readings, were recorded during, before and after meditation. Oxygen samples were taken as well as blood samples. The subjects meditated for between 20 and 30 minutes following a pre-meditation period of relaxation which also was between 20 and 30 minutes. Twenty to 30 minutes after the meditation period, tests were discontinued.

The brain waves recorded by the EEG showed

similar patterns to those of the Zen monks recorded in the Japanese study already mentioned; that is, a high alpha level descending to an average 8 or 9 cycles per second and concluding with the appearance of theta waves for a few subjects. Again, as with other tests, a decreased metabolic rate was manifested in decreased use of oxygen. The amount of oxygen used fell from a pre-meditation rate of 251 cubic centimeters to an average 211 cc. during meditation. In the period following meditation, it gradually rose to 242 cc. The amount of carbon dioxide given off showed a parallel decrease from 219 cc. to 187 cc. followed by a gradual return to pre-meditation elimination quantities. Shallower respiration during meditation used an average of one liter of air a minute. The breathing involved was spontaneous rather than controlled. Resistance of the skin to electrical current increased, in some cases by as much as four times the usual amount. Skin resistance is sometimes but not always associated with nervous tension. An increased resistance indicates a greater tolerance for pain.

The effect of meditation on the blood pressure is a significant one. In the pre-meditation period of TM, Wallace and Benson recorded that the blood pressure levels of all their subjects fell and remained rather lower than average during meditation and post-meditation periods. The average systolic blood pressure was recorded at 106 milliliters and diastolic pressure at 57 ml. This was accompanied by a slightly increased, but not abnormally high, blood acidity level, an indication of changes in the rate of blood metabolism. According to Wallace and Benson, the flow of blood in the forearm increased by 32 percent. However, University of Tubingen studies record a much higher increase. The increased flow of blood in the arm appears to be the reason for the rather drastic drop in blood lactate levels observed during pre-meditation, which continued to fall by amounts four times as great as those normal for ordinary states of relaxation. It seems, again according to Wallace and Benson, that here oxygen metabolism increases because the oxygen is being sent out more quickly to the muscles due to increased blood flow. Increased oxygen metabolism lessens the body's need for blood lactate, which is carried by the system known as anaerobic metabolism.

There is a definite correlation between blood lactate levels and stress. Patients suffering from anxiety neuroses, for instance, show particularly high levels of lactate. The research of Pitts and McClure at Washington University School of Medicine proves that raising the level of blood lactate will produce chronic anxiety symptoms even in normally placid subjects. High levels of lactate are present in hypertensives also. It is therefore hardly surprising that during the relaxing process of meditation blood lactate levels are decreased.

Meditation and Health

Dmitri Kanellakos, a Stanford research engineer, reports that not only does Transcendental Meditation decrease tension, both physical and mental, and produce a state of tranquillity in its practitioners, but it also increases their energy and capacity for concentrated effort. Its implications for use in the improvement of health are quite profound. Wallace has some statistics derived from a questionnaire sent out to 394 transcendental meditators. The information he received back told of generally improved health, notably in those areas most affected by stress. For instance, 333 of the respondents confess to an improved state of mental health, 29 mention they have fewer headaches and 7 that their high blood pressure had been reduced since they started to meditate.

Much attention has been given to the effect TM has had on young practitioners, many of whom were heavily involved with drugs before they began meditation but who, in the course of time, found that they no longer needed or desired drugs. One study on the effects of TM on drug usage was undertaken by W.Q. Winquist at UCLA, using 484 subjects between the ages of 15 and 30. Thirty percent of these subjects had been regular drug users, taking narcotics in both categories, hard and soft, for at least 3 months before starting to meditate. Winquist's findings indicated that 49 percent of the drug users had discontinued drug use, the majority of these reporting that drugs were no longer pleasurable or necessary.

Wallace and Benson made a more thorough investigation of the effects of TM on drug abuse. To discover if and how their subjects' abuse of drugs had diminished, they divided the questionnaire sent out to 1950 meditators into separate time frames. It was found that 6 months before becoming involved with TM about 80 percent of the sample who answered the questionnaire had used marihuana, 48 percent had used hallucinogenic drugs, 30 percent amphetamines and 27 percent barbiturates. After six months of meditating, 37 percent were still using marihuana, but as time progressed there was a steady decline until, after 22 months, only one meditator still was using this drug heavily, with 12 percent using it occasionally. In the case of

LSD, 11 percent of the meditators formerly involved with this drug still reported that they used it. Other figures are equally significant.

The most significant medical uses of meditation lie in the reduction of the symptoms of high blood pressure and in the removal of stress-related symptoms, such as headaches, migraine, disorders of the digestive tract, insomnia and nervous tension. Meditation is not a remedy which physicians or psychologists can prescribe to a patient. The use of meditation depends entirely upon the character of a patient, his willingness to subject himself to a discipline.

We suggest that the practice of meditation, of whatever sort, is somewhat like the taking of a regular fast. Because, superficially, it is not a direct medical remedy for the improvement of health, many people who are not attracted to its philosophical applications will discount its importance. We believe that part of meditation's importance is that it requires the individual to make a choice. By using meditation, by using regular fasting techniques, by becoming aware to the fullest degree of the circumstances occurring within ourselves as well as in the outside world, we can improve our ability to deal with some of those problems which contribute to the lowering of the quality of life and the diminishment of good health in our culture.

The type of meditation chosen is a personal thing. One should choose and use a type compatible to himself and his needs. One should *not* force himself into a method of meditation merely because someone else suggested it. To be successful, meditation must be a relaxing "letting go" process, not a "pushing through" process.

In the field of scientific endeavor, we are beginning to see a growing concern with and interest in the nature of human consciousness. Many highly qualified scientific researchers of every discipline from biochemistry to engineering are beginning to take an interest in activities such as meditation which were formerly considered to be of little value or interest. What we see, in fact, is an amelioration to some degree of the alienation which until now always existed between logical, scientifically based deductive ways of looking at the universe and at life and its more intuitive, non-linear aspects. It is now possible to scientifically test the basis of a seemingly irrational experience and to see how far experience is based on deductively provable occurrences. It is hoped that this new attitude will bring about a more optimistic, healthier, less stressful quality of life in the future.

Bibliography

Akhilananda—*Hindu Psychology: Its Meaning for the West* (New York: Harper, 1956)

Akshige, Yoshikara—A Historical Survey of Psychological Studies on Zen (*Kyushu Psychol. Studies, 5,* 1956)

Allison, J—Respiratory Changes during the Practice of the Technique of Transcendental Meditation (*Lancet, 7651,* 1970)

Anand, B. et al.—Some Aspects of EEG Studies in Yogis (*Electroenceph. & Clin. Neuro., 13,* 1961)

Anand, B. et al.—Studies on Shri Ramanand Yogi during His Stay in an Air-tight Box (*Indian Journal of Medical Research, 49,* 1961)

Bagchi, B.K. and Wenger, M.—Electrophysiological Correlates of Some Yogi Exercises (*Electroenceph. & Clin. Neuro., 7,* 1957)

Benson, H.—Yoga for Drug Abuse (*N.E.J. Med.,* November 1969)

Datey, K. et al.—Shavasan, a Yogic Exercise in the Management of Hypertension (*Angiology, 9,* 1969)

Deikman, A.— Experimental Meditation (*J. Nervous & Mental Diseases, 136,* 1963)

Deikman, A.—Deautomatization and the Mystic Experience (*Psychiatry, 29,* 1966)

Deikman, A.—Implications of Experimentally Induced Meditative Contemplation (*J. Nervous & Mental Diseases, 142,* 1966)

Fadiman, J.—The Council Grove Conference on Altered States of Consciousness (*J. Humanistic Psych., 9,* 1969)

Forem, J.—*Transcendental Meditation* (New York: Dutton, 1963)

Hoenig, J.—Medical Research on Yoga (*Confinia Psychiatrica, 11,* 1968)

James, William—*The Varieties of Religious Experience* (New York: Mentor Books, 1968)

Kasamatsu, A. and Hirai, T.—Science of Zazen (*Psychologia, 6,* 1963)

Kasamatsu, A. and Hirai, T.—An Electroencephalographic Study of Zen Meditation (Zazen) (*Folia Psychiat. Neurol., 20,* 1966)

Le Shan, Lawrence—Physicists and Mystics: Similarities in World View (*J. Transpers. Psychol., 1,* 1969)

Marechal, J.—*Studies in the Phychology of the Mystics* (Albany, N.Y.: Magi, 1964)

Moller, H.—Affective Mysticism in Western Civilization (*Psychoanalytical Review, 52,* 1965)

Naranjo, Claudio and Ornstein, Robert E.—*On the Psychology of Meditation* (New York: Viking, 1971)

Needleman, Jacob—*The New Religions* (New York: Doubleday, 1970)

Nyaponika, Thera—*The Heart of Buddhist Meditation* (London: Rider, 1962)

Okeima, T. et al.—The EEG of Yoga and Zen Practitioners (*Electroenceph. & Clin. Neuro., 51,* 1967)

Ornstein, Robert E. (ed.)—*The Nature of Human Consciousness* (San Francisco: W.H. Freeman, 1973)

Pearce, J.—*The Crack in the Cosmic Egg* (New York: Julian Press, 1951)

Silverman, J.—A Paradigm for the Study of Altered States of Consciousness (*Br. J. Psychiat., 114,* 1968)

Suzuki, D.T.—*The Training of the Zen Buddhist Monk* (New York: University Books, 1959)

Tart, Charles T. (ed.)—*Altered States of Consciousness* (New York: Wiley, 1969)

Wallace, R.K.—Psychological Effects of TM (*Science, 167,* 1970)

Wallace, R. et al.—A Wakeful Hypermetabolic Physiological State (*Am. J. Physiol., 221,* 1971)

White, J. (ed.) *The Highest State of Consciousness* (New York: Doubleday, 1971)

Woods, J.—*The Yoga System of Patanjali* (Cambridge, Mass.: Harvard University Press, 1914)

PART III

Know Your Body

In the first two parts of this book, we have suggested that a great deal may be learned from ancient traditions such as fasting and meditation and that through their use we may improve our level of health and become more able to deal with some of the exigencies of modern life which are in part responsible for poor health. We attempted to show that a sound scientific basis underlies such regimens, as well as to suggest that their use, along with biofeedback training, may teach us to know our bodies better.

When a phrase such as "know your body" is used, what is often meant is a purely intuitive knowledge, a knowledge which, as neurological research is proving, is a very real factor but has been blunted considerably by civilization. We can no longer use our basic animal instincts in the way they were used by our remote ancestors or by many so-called primitive peoples today, who knew and know how to maintain their health, what and how to eat, without benefit of the scientific knowledge we now possess. Bearing in mind that primitive peoples of the past were dependent on a favorable environment, we can say that their survival was based on a knowledge at first perhaps instinctual, then traditional. A situation where people live close to the earth, totally involved in the cycle of nature, the movement of the seasons, the nature of the hunt and later the growth of the crops is indeed a far cry from our modern civilization. Even today's more primitive, land-based groups are to some extent influenced by modern urban traditions and thereby, too often, impoverished.

However, modern scientific endeavor has opened up new worlds of knowledge to us. While doing so, as we have attempted to suggest, it has started to close the gap between knowledge that was thought of as "intuitive" and knowledge that was thought of as "logical," to show that they are not mutually incompatible. Likewise, fascinating discoveries are being made about the functions of the body and mind from which all can benefit. To know our bodies can be a specifically factual pursuit as well as a matter of observation. The discoveries which have been made in all areas of biology, biochemistry, physiology, neurology, medicine, even cybernetics and engineering, have opened up new worlds for research and understanding.

This kind of knowledge is, we believe, vital at a time when the world is threatened with crises, at a time when pollution has become a threat to all life, when there is doubt whether the planet can grow enough food to sustain a multiplying population, when disease is not only not being conquered but on the increase. If we are to learn how to cope with these problems, one of the first steps for concerned citizens is, quite logically, to understand the functioning of the human system and what it needs to maintain itself.

This part therefore sets out, somewhat simply, to supply the background to the book. For some readers it will no doubt be redundant but, in this era of specialization, many readers, while understanding basic ideas like the functions of the body organs, may perhaps be confused by certain terms and have inadequate knowledge of some of the subjects covered. This, of course, is hardly surprising in areas where specialists themselves are confused. Much new work is being done, for example, on the function of hormones, the research on cellular function is far from complete, new vitamins are still being discovered, and neurologists have only recently begun to understand the exact functioning of the brain. For the lay person, much of this knowledge is difficult to understand even when it is available. However, we believe a basic knowledge is essential and in this part we try to assemble some of its basic components, as well as to suggest further reading to supplement it.

Cells

All living organisms, all plant life and all animal life from the smallest unicellular creatures like protozoa to the most complex of the mammals, Homo sapiens, are composed of chemical elements the molecules of which, arranged in a multiplicity of ways, are the building blocks of all known existing matter. In most living matter the chemical molecules form primary units called cells (although some organisms, such as slime molds, are not composed of cells) which combine to form the organism as a whole.

To describe the cell as a basic unit does not imply that it is a simple one. The structure of cells is immensely complicated and sets the pattern for the larger organism. The individual cell has the same needs whether it is the sole component of a simple organism like the amoeba or whether it is one of millions of tissue cells in a human being. To survive, the cell needs to consume other matter, in order to maintain, repair and renew itself, to supply itself and the rest of the body with the essential tools for growth and energy.

Individual cells are adapted to specific needs of the organism they help form. Most are very small units indeed. They are measured in microns and angstroms, the micron being one thousandth of a millimeter and the angstrom 1/10,000,000 of a millimeter. The tissue cells of the body cling together and this determines their various shapes, while a free cell such as the amoeba continually changes shape.

Cells are surrounded by the plasma membrane, the outer wall of the cell which determines its shape and keeps the internal cellular fluids intact. The interior of the cell is made up of the cytoplasm and the nucleus. It is the nucleus which controls the functioning of the individual cell and ensures the survival of the organism. New cells must constantly be made as old cells die off. This is effected by means of cell division, wherein daughter cells are formed which exactly resemble the parent cells, a complex process which entails the passing on of exact information in order that the new cells should not deviate. It is only recently that this information-duplicating process was located as the function of the molecular acid known as deoxyribonucleic acid—DNA. Biochemically speaking, DNA is composed of sugars named deoxyribose and a phosphate-based acid with traces of four other acids, adenine, thiamine, guanine and cytosine. In the nucleus, DNA usually combines with several sorts of proteins. Although DNA is the carrier of genetic information which is necessary for cell duplication, this information is relayed to the new cells by another nucleic acid, RNA, ribonucleic acid which exists in both the nucleus and the cytoplasm.

The function of the cytoplasm is to obtain food and break it down for use by the rest of the cell and to release its energy to enable the work of the cell to continue.

The fluid of the cytoplasm is composed of several salts and of small particles called mitochondria and microsomes. In the mitochondria are enzymes, those proteinaceous compounds which act as catalysts to break down the molecules of fats and carbohydrates (a process which will be described elsewhere in this chapter). Thousands of enzymes may exist in each cell. Most cellular enzymes are high in phosphates, the most important of them being adenosine triphosphate, essential to the formation of energy through the burning of food molecules into carbon dioxide and water molecules.

The microsomes are mostly concerned with building proteins, the building materials of the cell. To do this they make use of the energy being formed by the mitochondria. In a complex organism only certain cells, those of the glands especially, are specialized for synthesizing proteins. The cytoplasm of such cells contains ribosomes and the RNA of the ribosomes functions mainly to synthesize protein.

Proteins

Proteins are very complex and their molecules are relatively large. They are very important because they compose nearly half the total weight of the individual cell and of the organism as a whole. Proteins are the building materials of the body. Our bones, muscles, blood, skin, hair and internal organs are mostly protein.

Each protein is made up of amino acids which are arranged in a chain, the order of which is slightly different in each protein. Each amino acid has a slightly different chemical composition apart from the basic structure, which consists of one nitrogen and two hydrogen atoms. Protein amino acids are constantly reforming and making different chemical bonds to join together in a new way. This is what happens during the process of digestion when protein molecules are broken down in the cells by the action of enzymes.

The Digestive System

The digestive system is the process by which all foods, proteins, carbohydrates and fats, are broken down to be used by the body: proteins for building up the cells and tissues, carbohydrates and fats for providing energy and protective warmth. All these foods must be broken down into their constituent molecules and then reassembled.

In a unicellular animal such as the amoeba, one of the group called protozoans, digestion is of the simplest kind. The amoeba does not eat, but flows around a piece of food matter which must therefore be smaller than the animal itself. Once within the cytoplasm of the amoeba, the food is worked on by the enzymes of the mitochondria until it is absorbed and utilized. This type of digestion serves as a model in a simplified form for the many processes which take place in the much more complex human digestive system.

The basic plan of the alimentary canal and the associated organs of the human digestive tract can be observed even in an earthworm. The digestive tract of a worm is really a tube with two openings, one for ingestion, one for the excretion of the unused products of digestion. In worms, as in the much more complicated human system, the main agents of the changes which occur during the process of digestion are enzymes.

Enzymes

Enzymes are made up of proteins, or more precisely of about 500 different amino acid residues. Enzymes are most often referred to as "catalysts," which means that they speed up the necessary chemical reactions which must take place for digestion to occur. They do not in themselves cause these reactions, but they do speed up the change which might otherwise occur too slowly for life to continue. Catalysts, it should be emphasized, are not themselves changed by the reaction which they help to create. Enzymes accelerate reaction speed considerably, causing between a hundred and five million molecules of a substrate to react per minute. (A substrate is any food capable of being acted on by an enzyme.) Despite the speed of some enzymic reactions, none of them is complete in itself. Food must be acted upon by several different enzymes before is can be used.

There are several different kinds of reactions which enzymes can cause. Hydrolytic enzymes split apart the molecules of a substrate and incorporate the pieces with water. This is the first reaction which occurs in a piece of food as it enters the digestive system. Other enzymes control oxidation. That is, they help the body to form energy by burning food molecules through the addition of atoms of oxygen and the removal of hydrogen atoms. Another process through which enzymes split molecules is accomplished without water molecules. One of the final reactions which enzymes cause is the transfer of atoms of one molecule to those of another. This process takes place when amino acids are re-formed in protein synthesis.

There are certain other substances called coenzymes which help enzymes to perform their functions. Adenosine triphosphate (ATP) is considered a coenzyme. Another example is nicotinamide-adenine dinucleotide (NAD). There are, of course, many more but these two are the ones most commonly referred to. Their main action seems to lie in storing energy or allowing it to be released. Vitamins are coenzymes and many coenzymes include vitamins in their makeup. For instance, riboflavin is important in the process of oxidation. Substances called inorganic ions are also coenzymes. Ions are substances which can be either positively or negatively charged with electricity. Sodium is a positively charged ion, for example, and potassium, a negatively charged ion. Ions can react with amino acids in a way that causes changes in the shape of the protein molecule and aids protein synthesis.

Some ions, like other substances, hinder the action of enzymes. Metal ions like mercury and lead prevent enzymes from functioning and thus are exceedingly dangerous. This inhibitory factor is what has created public concern over the use of mercury, lead and many non-ion organic chemicals contained in agricultural insecticides, for example. Similarly, nerve gases inhibit the action of those enzymes necessary for the transmission of nerve impulses.

Enzymes are not only extremely complex chemically, they are also, like all proteins, very delicate and their action is easy to inhibit. They can be destroyed by heating, dehydration or an excess of water. New enzymes must continually be formed for the body to continue functioning. To maintain cellular balance, old enzymes have to be removed and new ones continually incorporated. The enzyme-making agents of the cells are the nucleic acids which are involved in the process of protein synthesis as well as the transmission of the genetic code. In fact, protein synthesis and the carrying of genetic traits are intimately related since a model of the protein molecule, whether of enzymes or other proteins, is carried by the RNA of the ribosomes, which are then able to duplicate the specific order of the amino acids. Only the particular type of protein for which the RNA of a particular ribosome carries a pattern can be manufactured by that messenger RNA. Therefore, it follows that each cell involved in protein and enzyme synthesis requires hundreds of thousands of different RNA molecules.

Enzymes and Digestion

The Mouth

Food is first broken down by chewing. Careful chewing is important because the food should be mixed well with saliva, a substance which is composed of 98 percent water and a viscous substance called mucin which carries the first of the enzymes the food will come into contact with. This is ptyalin, or salivary amylase, a hydrolyzing enzyme which breaks up starch molecules, beginning the process of splitting the glucose molecules into sugars and dextrins.

Saliva, of which about half a liter is secreted during the day, keeps the mouth lubricated and turns the food into a semi-liquid ball called a bolus which can then be swallowed easily. When the bolus of food is swallowed, the food is forced into the first part of the alimentary canal, the esophagus, which is 9 or 10 inches long and nearly an inch wide, lined with circular muscles. The muscles of the esophagus contract in order to force the food down into the stomach. This series of contracting movements is called peristalsis.

The Stomach

The stomach is a muscular, saclike organ, the widest part of the alimentary canal. It lies just below the diaphragm where the esophagus ends in the cardiac sphincter. Sphincter is the name given to a circular muscle which is in a state of almost constant contraction. The cardiac sphincter is so called because of its closeness to the heart. As the bolus approaches, the cardiac sphincter relaxes and the food enters the stomach, where it will stay, in human beings, for a maximum of three hours.

The mucous membrane which lines the stomach is studded with numerous minute glands which secrete the gastric or stomach juices. This juice contains about 0.5 percent hydrochloric acid, a strong inorganic acid. The presence of the acid was discovered in 1824 and caused much speculation about how the delicate tissues of the stomach could remain unharmed. The answer appears to be that the stomach wall is protected by the antacid mucus secretions. The protection is not always perfect, even so, for if any section of the stomach wall becomes irritated by the erosive gastric juices, a sore, or gastric ulcer, forms. This condition is liable to occur when nervous tension causes the secretion of hyperacid stomach juices. The normal acid state of the stomach is however not as undesirable as some commercial aspirin manufacturers make it appear, because hydrochloric acid provides the enzyme pepsin with the environment it needs to work in, thereby helping break down some of the molecular bonds of proteins. Most enzymes function best when a certain amount of acid is present. Pepsin splits protein molecules into polypeptides, that is, into fragments of protein each containing a fairly large number of amino acids joined together. It thus begins the process of hydrolyzation, but only attacks peptide bonds between some amino acids and not others.

Hydrochloric acid also helps to hydrolyze the enzyme pepsin itself. For pepsin is made in the cells in the form of pepsinogen. Once the action of hydrochloric acid has converted a few molecules of the cellular protein pepsinogen into pepsin, then the rest of the work can be done by the pepsin thus formed. Such a process is known as autocatalysis.

The gastric juices gradually reduce most of the food in the stomach to a fluid substance, the chyme, which is sterile because the acidity of the stomach juices has killed off most of the bacteria originally present in the food.

The Small Intestine

This is where the major work of digestion takes place. The small intestine is about 1½ to 2 inches in diameter at the point at which it is joined to the stomach and becomes narrower as it increases in length. The small intestine in human beings is also about 20 feet in length and fills most of the abdominal cavity. The first part of the small intestine is the duodenum, which is somewhat vulnerable to the development of ulcers in its lining because of the impact of the acidic chyme.

To counteract the effects of the chyme, two glands secrete neutralizing juices into the duodenum. The first of these glands is the pancreas. The pancreas passes about 0.7 liters of fluid a day into the duodenum through the pyloric sphincter, a duct which opens into the duodenum about an inch and a half below the stomach. Pancreatic juice contains sodium bicarbonate to neutralize the acid and number of enzymes, which need a neutral environment rather than an acidic one to function in.

Pancreatic amalyse or amylopsin is an enzyme which continues the work of ptyalin in breaking down starches, converting them into polysaccharides which are long chainlike molecules of sugar, and maltose, a disaccharide (i.e., having two molecules of sugar as opposed to many).

The enzyme lipase is also contained in the pancreatic juice. "Lipase" has the same root, "lip," as "lipid," or fat, and it is upon fat that lipase acts. Lipase is a hydrolyzing enzyme which breaks the fat molecules into glycerol and free fatty acids. In the course of this reaction, intermediate substances called monoglycerides and diglycerides are formed. They are necessary because, since fats are not water-soluble, lipase cannot easily break down the fat molecules until the formation of the mono- and diglycerides. Combining with the salts secreted by the bile, which act on the fat globules in much the same way as soap, these intermediates make it possible for fats to be broken down by pancreatic lipase in a watery environment.

Bile is secreted by the liver to the duodenum at the rate of about 0.5 liters a day by way of the hepatic duct. Far more is secreted than can be used and has to be stored in the sac of the gall bladder which lies just below the lower right lobe of the four-lobed liver. Most of the function of the bile lies in the secretion of the neutralizing bile-salts. Bile contains no enzymes.

The most important pancreatic enzymes are trypsin, chymotrypsin and carboxypeptidase which continue and complete the protein-splitting work of pepsin. Just as with pepsin, the cells first secrete these three enzymes in the inactive forms called trypsinogen, chymotrypsinogen and procarboxypeptidase, which then have to be hydrolyzed before they can function. Trypsin is the enzyme which effects this process, having been partly formed by another protein-splitting enzyme, enterokinase, small amounts of which are secreted by the pancreatic juice. The three enzymes hydrolyze different amino acid residues and help the protein molecule to break down into smaller and smaller pieces.

By the time the chyme has reached the next part of the small intestine, the jejunum, the actual digestive process has been completed. The enzymes secreted by the cells which line the intestinal walls break up whatever parts of molecules remain. They break the digested matter into substances suitable for absorption directly into the tiny blood vessels which also line the walls of the small intestine. From there, the digested matter is relayed into the general circulation of the blood so that it can be taken back to the cells to be used as building material for the fats, carbohydrates and proteins from which the tissues of the body are constructed. In this way are processed the raw materials of the energy which enables the body to perform its various tasks.

Assimilation

In the lining of the small intestine are set fine hairlike projections called villi which set up a churning motion to keep the chyme constantly moving. At the base of each villus in the intestinal glands, groups of cells secrete those enzymes which break down protein for absorption. There are fragments of protein molecules left over after the pancreatic enzymes have done their work and these are attacked by enzymes called peptidases. To be absorbed, proteins must be broken down into single amino acids. The carbohydrates have been broken down into poly- and disaccharides. The enzyme maltase reduces the disaccharide maltose to glucose. Sucrase forms glucose and fructose from sucrose, the molecules of ordinary table sugar. The compound molecules of milk sugar, lactose, are reduced by the enzyme lactase into glucose and galactose. Fat molecules, broken down into glycerol and fatty acids, are not as easily soluble as the other materials and they tend to be absorbed in the form of tiny globules which eventually also pass into the blood stream.

The Liver

The end products of carbohydrate and protein digestion enter the liver by way of a network of capillaries and veins leading from the villi. The nutritive blood is filtered in the small veins of the liver, the sinusoids, to rid it of any debris such as bacteria remaining from the processes of digestion and absorption. Excess glucose and amino acids are removed by cells bordering the sinusoids, the glucose being re-formed into glycogen to be stored until needed in the form of glucose again. Any fructose or galactose surviving at this stage of assimilation is converted first into glucose, then glycogen.

The liver allows only a small amount of glucose to re-enter the blood stream. This glucose will be assimilated and converted into energy. Between meals, the stored glycogen is gradually changed by the liver into glucose and released to the blood stream in the same way. If, when the liver is filled to capacity with as much glycogen as it can store, glucose continues to reach the liver—which is what occurs when we overeat—the excess glucose can only be turned into fat. Fat, unlike glycogen, can be stored in indefinite quantities. A similar thing happens to excess protein, which is formed out of the store of amino acids by the liver.

Vitamins are also stored in the liver, Vitamins A and D in the liver fat and Vitamin B_{12}, which aids in the formation of red blood cells. Among the chemical changes performed by the liver are those concerned with detoxification. Hemoglobin, the red-colored protein occurring in red blood cells which carries oxygen around the body, is broken down in the liver. From its breakdown, bilirubin, the pigment which colors bile, is secreted. It is a waste product, partly expelled by the blood as urine, which absorbs a little of it in the process. This is why both blood plasma and urine are a similar light straw or amber color. If too much bile pigment gets into the blood, it will produce jaundice, with its characteristic yellowish-green coloration of skin, mucus and eye whites.

Besides the bile pigment and cholesterol, the fatty substance which the bile is particularly rich in, the liver dissolves those chemicals which cannot be used for energy or absorbed by the cells and prepares them for excretion. Nitrogen left over from protein metabolism is formed into urea with the addition of ammonia and carbon dioxide. They make the substances in the blood plasma known as albumin and globulin, as well as fibrinogen and prothrombin, which are essential for blood clotting.

If there is an influx of alien chemicals into the liver, it is likely to become overstrained, possibly suffering permanent damage. When this happens, the damaged liver cells are gradually replaced by fat and connective tissue, a condition known as cirrhosis of the liver.

Elimination

After the process of assimilation there are still particles of food left over. If digestion is effective, all substrates should have been absorbed leaving only cellulose, the fibrous part of plants which cannot be acted upon by the enzymes present in human beings. Animals which eat mostly grass, such as cows, are able to utilize cellulose only by keeping it in their stomachs for a long time and digesting it more than once. Cellulose and connective tissue, which cannot remain long enough in the human digestive system to be acted upon by enzymes, form feces which gather in the colon or large intestine. As they go through the colon, the large amounts of water which the body has used in the processes of digestion and absorption are gradually eliminated, so that as the body prepares to excrete the feces they become harder.

The large intestine is formed out of the three sections known as the ascending, transverse and descending colon. The first part of the ascending colon has a vestigial appendage called the vermiform appendix which appears to be a leftover from the process of evolution. In herbivorous animals, the cecum, from which the appendix extends, serves as a place of storage and fermentation. In human beings, the appendix may cause trouble if some small piece of undigested food strays into it, and irritates the tissues to the point of rupture.

Feces contain a great number of the bacteria which multiply in the large intestine, most of which are harmless, but a few of which may be virulent. It is the contamination of water reservoirs by harmful fecal bacteria that spreads diseases such as dysentery, cholera and typhoid fever. Modern plumbing has done much to avert such contamination.

It is important that the diet contain adequate amounts of cellulose and connective tissue which are easily excreted as "roughage" and take with them the more harmful waste products. If the body is unable to rid itself of its waste products, toxemia may result. This will also occur if the system is forced to ingest an abnormally high amount of substances which cannot be used either to maintain the tissues or to form energy. Not only can toxins not be utilized by the body, but their effect on the organs is extremely dangerous. The detoxifying capacities of the liver if overabused will result in dysfunction and death of cells. As has already been mentioned, certain substances which are commonly used in agricultural insecticides have an inhibitory or destructive effect on the enzymes, coenzymes and vitamins without which food cannot be digested. Commonly used toxins which are often ingested are some hormones used in the feed of livestock, insecticides, dyes, and other substances containing such chemicals as sodium nitrate, sulphur dioxide, sodium fluoride and mercury. The proliferation of such chemicals in easily ingestible foodstuffs is alarming and is, of course, one of the ills successfully remedied by fasting.

The Kidneys and Excretion

Not all waste matter exits by way of the feces. Some waste matter enters the blood, as is the case with urea. The kidneys carry out what is essentially a filtering process by which waste matter can be eliminated from the blood. Kidneys contain around a million filtering tubes called nephrons, through which at any given time about a quarter of the total blood supply may be passing in order to be cleansed of impurities. The blood arrives in the kidneys by way of the renal artery which branches off from the aorta, the main artery of the heart. The renal artery splits into smaller arterioles, each of which subdivides into smaller capillaries which recombine and redivide, finally arriving to feed the kidneys. The blood passes out of the kidneys by the renal vein to the inferior vena cava. While this process is going on, water, ions and molecules of urea are able to pass into the nephrons, the first section of which is known as Bowman's Capsule (after the British surgeon who first described it). Bowman's Capsule leads into the convoluted tubule, as it is accurately named, where useful material can be reabsorbed. After this, the solution which drains through the rest of the tubule, divided into the proximal convoluted tubule and distal convoluted tubule which are connected by a long straight narrow tube called Henle's Loop, becomes more and more concentrated. About 80 percent of the water and ions that pass through Bowman's Capsule are reabsorbed in the proximal convoluted tubule.

Because water must not be wasted, the body reabsorbs about 99 percent of it, aided by the hormone ADH, which is secreted by the pituitary glands. Only the minimum amount of fluid necessary to dissolve the waste products is allowed to escape from the body if this hormone is functioning correctly. If the hormone function is impaired, urination becomes both heavy and very dilute, leading to the diseases of poluria and diabetes insipidus which can at first be rectified by drinking large amounts of water. Eventually, however, the disease leads to kidney failure and a concentration of urea in the blood known as uremia, often fatal.

Other kidney damage is caused when blood pressure through the kidneys is reduced or raised. If reduced, the kidney reacts by producing a substance called renin meant to counteract the effects of the lowered pressure by causing greater contraction of the arterioles and increasing the level of blood pressure. If the blood pressure is too high, the arteries thicken and renal damage ensues as in the disease of hypertension.

Obesity

Many diseases, such as hypertension, diabetes mellitus and other forms of heart and kidney disease, are caused by the accumulation of so great a quantity of fat that organic function becomes disturbed. The chief functions of fat are insulation against the cold and protection for the organs. Fat is stored in the cells of connective tissue, where it forms little globules. It collects in particularly large amounts in the membraneous sac called the omentum which surrounds the stomach. The stored fat is called adipose tissue and accounts for about 15 percent of the weight of an average person. Obesity is most commonly caused by overeating, but may also result from impaired hormonal activity.

Hormones

Hormones are fairly simple chemical compounds which have a regulatory effect on the bodily functions they control: among others, metabolism, sexual activity, pregnancy and growth. Despite their relative simplicity, they are not yet properly understood. They are produced by eight different glands of which the pituitary is the most important in that it is responsible for overall hormone regulation.

The pituitary gland is situated at the base of the skull. Its front, or anterior, part is made of three types of cells: the acidophils, which produce growth hormone and regulate milk production in pregnant women; the basophils, which secrete hormones to stimulate the hormone functions of other glands; and the chromophobes.

The hypothalamus is part of the posterior pituitary gland and can be considered as part of the brain. It produces two hormones: ADH (Antidiuretic hormone), which affects the kidneys already discussed, and oxytocin, which is activated during pregnancy.

The thyroid gland, which is on either side of the larynx, produces hormones like thyroxin which are metabolic regulators. If a person is hyperthyroid, metabolic rate increases alarmingly and the patient loses weight, feels hot and sweaty, and has an unusually fast blood circulation and pulse rate. Thyroxin also affects growth and brain function. If a thyroxin deficiency exists from birth, the child will be mentally and physically retarded. A deficiency developing later in life causes the patients to put on weight, slow down physically and mentally and feel excessively cold because mucus develops under the skin. Metabolism becomes extremely slow. This condition is called myxedema. Another thyroid hormone is calcitonin, which lowers the level of calcium in the blood.

The parathyroid glands also affect calcium and phosphate levels. They stimulate the bone cells to release calcium and the kidneys to release phosphate. If the parathyroid hormones are overactive, they can cause bone damage and impaired kidney function by increasing the amount of calcium in the blood.

The adrenal glands are situated at the upper portions of the kidneys. They produce two hormones which activate the sympathetic nervous system, adrenalin and nonadrenalin. The sympathetic nerves go to the heart, blood, intestines and bladder, and release adrenalin and nonadrenalin. These can cause quickened pulse rate, rise in blood pressure and other expressions of excitation or fear. Acetylcholine, a hormone, affects the parasympathetic nervous system and particularly activates the sweat glands, which are located in the inner part of the adrenals, the medulla. The outer part, or adrenal cortex, releases corticoid (or corticosteroid) hormones. One of these, aldosterone, regulates the amount of salt in the body. Another, cortisol (or hydrocortisone), is responsible for the regulation of water. They both regulate the metabolism of foods and help counteract stress.

Insulin

Diabetes was much discussed in the part of the book dealing with fasting. Diabetes mellitus is caused by a deficiency of insulin, which is made in the glands of the pancreas known as the Islets of Langerhans. Insulin, which is made of protein, regulates the amount of glucose in the blood. When there is a deficiency of insulin, too much glucose is made, and it appears in the urine. The whole metabolism is impaired. Fats are broken down in excessive amounts, and it is this which causes the production of the acids called ketones which are a by-product of diabetes. Along with the glucose, much water and salts are excreted with the urine, causing dehydration. Mild diabetes can be controlled sometimes by reducing the carbohydrates taken in the diet, but when the disease is severe, insulin is injected intravenously to prevent the patient from going into a coma and dying.

Blood

The blood carries foodstuffs, minerals and hormones to the cells, transports oxygen all over the body, and helps remove waste products. The liquid part of the blood is called plasma, and the solid parts are divided into three types of cells. The red blood cells contain hemoglobin, the red pigment, a proteinaceous substance which contains iron and is involved in oxygen transportation. Red cells are called erythrocytes and have no nuclei. If there is a deficiency of hemoglobin, anemia occurs. One of the causes of hemoglobin deficiency is a lack of sufficient iron in the cells. Lack of certain vitamins, particularly Vitamin C, folic acid and B_{12}, also is contributory. In severe or pernicious anemia, food is not absorbed properly.

There are five types of white blood cells, but they are known collectively as leucocytes. These cells are involved in combating foreign bodies such as bacteria and disposing of dead or damaged cells. This is done by a process of cellular digestion called phagocytis, which means cell-eating. When red blood cells are eaten, which happens about every 90 days in man, this being the limit of their existence, the hemoglobin is digested and the iron saved to be used again.

The Heart and Blood Circulation

About five quarts of blood are contained within the human body, and it must be kept continually moving through several thousand miles of blood vessels which with the heart form the circulatory system, in order that the supply of oxygen and nutrients essential for the maintenance of life be conveyed by the blood to all parts of the body.

The circulatory system is controlled by the heart, an organ which acts like a pump to keep the blood circulating. About five inches long by 3½ inches wide, the eggplant-shaped heart is situated between the lungs. It is a muscular organ divided into four chambers. The two upper chambers, the right and left auricles, or atriums, are for storage, while the two lower chambers, the ventricles, pump the blood out to the rest of the body.

The blood vessels leading from the heart to the other areas of the body are called arteries. A powerful muscular contraction sends the blood flowing from the heart into the first of these arteries, the aorta, which leads directly out of the left ventricle. The aorta is the widest blood vessel of the body, about an inch in diameter at the point where it leaves the heart, though it narrows thereafter. The aorta divides into smaller arteries, which in turn subdivide into smaller and smaller arteries, rather like the branches of a tree.

As the arteries continue to divide into smaller and smaller vessels, they carry the blood all over the body. The smallest, thinnest-walled arteries, which are called arterioles, finally divide into threadlike capillaries. It is through the walls of the capillaries that new nutrient substances enter the blood stream. The capillaries lead to venules which are slightly larger in size and the venules lead into larger veins which carry the enriched blood back to the heart. The largest vein, the pulmonary vein, enters the heart at the right atrium. However, before the blood can be used by the heart it must go to the lungs, passing first through the right ventricle. From the lungs, the blood, now oxygen-enriched, enters the left atrium, passes down to the left ventricle and another cycle is about to begin.

The heart itself is nourished, not by the blood which passes through it, but by the blood fed to it from the two coronary vessels which also branch into many smaller arteries that lead into the heart.

Blood Pressure

As the blood is sent out by the heart it exerts pressure against the muscular walls of the arteries, which tighten or relax according to the amount of the flow. Usually the resistance of the arterial walls to the blood is lowered when the amount of blood from the heart is increased. When, for instance, more blood is needed by the stomach for the process of digestion, the arterioles in the walls of the stomach will relax so that more blood can flow into them. It is this activity of the arterioles which, with the regulating beat of the heart, determines blood pressure.

Blood pressure is measured in two ways. One, measured on the heart beat, is called systolic blood pressure, while the other, taken between heart beats, is called the diastolic blood pressure. A systolic blood pressure of between 100 and 140 millimeters of mercury is described as normal, as is a diastolic pressure of between 60 and 90 degrees. Blood pressure which is not contained within these limits is dangerous. Thus, not only high but also low blood pressure presents a problem, for if the diastolic pressure falls below 60 degrees, it is possible that the filtering function of the kidney will be impaired.

Blood pressure varies according to the demands of the body. It is lower when we are asleep than when we are awake. More blood is needed when the body is being exercised than when it is resting. The system is regulated by cells within the walls of the arteries, which work rather like a thermostat to regulate the pressure and maintain the blood flow at a suitable level. It is those baroceptor cells, as they are called, which signal the nervous system (which controls the circulation) to cause the arteriole muscles to relax or tighten.

Certain hormones also have some influence on blood pressure. Two examples are norepinephrine and epinephrine, which are secreted by the adrenal glands of the kidneys at times of emotional stress or unusual amounts of exercise. The effect these two hormones have on the blood pressure is one of constriction. Some chemical substances which are produced by hormones under normal conditions and others which are only activated in abnormal circumstances have the effect of strengthening or inhibiting blood response to nerve impulses. Those which strengthen response are known as pressor agents, while those which weaken the response and lower blood pressure are called depressor agents.

Blood Pressure and the Nervous System

The nervous system which controls the heart and circulatory system of the body is the autonomic nervous system. Unlike the central nervous system which controls all the actions of the body considered to be voluntary, such as the movement of the limbs, the autonomic nervous system is concerned with functions which up until recently were considered to be entirely automatic. Besides the circulatory system it controls, for example, digestion and respiration. The autonomic nervous system is divided into two subsystems, the sympathetic and the parasympathetic systems. The sympathetic nervous system becomes effective under stress conditions—physical exercise, mental effort and anxiety—while the parasympathetic functions under the opposite conditions—relaxation, sleep and meditation.

Nerve Cells

The nervous system, consisting of the brain, spinal cord and associated nervous cells, has been dealt with only slightly in Chapter 6 where some of the complexities of the brain were discussed, as well as the different functions of the several nervous systems.

The human brain is a structure of immense complexity weighing about three pounds in an adult. The two main areas of the brain are the cerebrum, consisting of four cavities, or ventricles, and the two frontal lobes of the cerebral cortex and the cerebellum, located just above the spinal cord. The outer layer of the cerebral cortex is grey and heavily convoluted. The inner tissue is white and made up of nerve fibers protected by fatty sheaths.

Nerve tissue consists of nerve cells, known as neurons, which are electrically charged, and connective tissue, known as neuroglia. Neurons vary in shape and size according to their location in the brain, but most of them have the same structure, composed of cell body, the dendrites—long branches or tails of protoplasm—and the axon, the part which conveys the information. The dendrites are not present in those neurons that handle receptor functions, such as vision, hearing and balance.

Cells are connected by the neuroglia, which come in three main types. Astrocytes exist in the grey matter and are concerned with nutrition and repair. Oligodendrocytes are smaller than astrocytes and produce the fatty sheaths which protect the nerve cells of the white matter. Microglia exist in all parts of the brain and their function is to ingest damaged brain cells.

The nerve fibers which extend from the brain and spinal cord to the voluntary muscles of the body are electrically insulated by a fatty covering called myelin which is produced by cells called Schwann cells. This makes the transmission of nerve impulses more rapid. Contractions which occur in muscles in response to nerve impulses are activated by the molecules of the proteins myosin and actin, together forming actomyosin, the energy being provided as usual by glucose. Nerve impulses themselves are both electrical and biochemical, and the ions of sodium and potassium present in nerve cells provide the electrical current. When the impulse arrives at its goal, it releases some of the hormone acetylcholine, which sets up a series of muscular reactions until destroyed by an enzyme called cholinesterase. The gross oversimplification of nerve impulses also applies to the process by which the messages reach the sensory receptors and involuntarily controlled functions described in Chapter 6. The brain is very highly specialized and as is the case with all the cells of the body, only specific groups of cells are specialized to deal with certain functions. Brain cells are different from other cells of the body in that they cannot reproduce themselves. Once a brain cell is destroyed, and of course brain cells are destroyed in vast quantities each day, it cannot be replaced. The brain is thus particularly vulnerable to incorrect nutrition (see Chapter 5) and to oxygen starvation.

Respiration

Air contains about 20 percent oxygen and 70 percent nitrogen, but it is oxygen that the cells require to produce energy in collaboration with the glucose and carbon dioxide which that energy releases.

Breathing is the process by which the body takes in oxygen and releases carbon dioxide. Air is taken into the human body through the nostrils which are lined with mucous membranes containing cells, called cilia, with hairlike projections. Their function is to remove impurities. Breathing can be effected through the mouth, too, of course, but the mouth is far less efficient due to the absence of the filtering mechanism of the cilia. The nasal passages lead into the epiglottis (also lined with cilia) which joins, then separates from, then crosses the esophagus and thence proceeds into the trachea, or windpipe. The trachea must be open at all times for so vital is oxygen to the body that if it is deprived of it for more than a few moments death will result. Just below the neck the trachea divides into the two branches of bronchi, each of which leads to a separate lung and in doing so divide and subdivide. The lungs fill most of the cavity of the thorax, the upper part of the body, and are somewhat dissimilar. The right lung is larger and divided into three lobes, while the left and smaller lung is divided into two lobes. The lobes are to some slight extent independent, for if one lobe becomes infected, it can be removed without too severe impairment.

The size of the lungs is unimportant because air is absorbed on the convoluted surface of the lungs which is protected by two layers of the membrane called the pleura. Only the smallest finest branches of the bronchioles are able to absorb air. These respiratory bronchioles lead into ducts covered with air sacs, each of which is covered with tiny cells, called alveoli, of which there are several million altogether. The alveoli have thin membranes which allow the free flow of air through the walls of the capillary blood vessels to which the alveoli are attached. The oxygen then combines with the hemoglobin of the red blood cells, thereby changing its color from purplish to bright red. The oxygenated blood can now leave the lungs for the left side of the heart.

Breathing is regulated by specialized nerve cells,

to which impulses are passed from the spinal cord. Breathing can also, of course, be voluntarily controlled, which to some extent is essential when speaking. However, it is the chemical state of the blood and the influence of the nervous system which substantially determine control of respiration. Carbon dioxide content, blood oxygenation level and acidity all have an influence. If the level of carbon dioxide produced by the energy cycle is raised, the nervous center of the respiratory system sends out messages which may cause discomfort to a person trying to control his breathing beyond a certain limit. Any attempt to hold the breath too long results in fainting at which point involuntary respiration takes over.

The organism can function with 70 percent of its oxygen needs. Oxygen supply can fail in various circumstances. Sufficient oxygen may not be available in the alveoli, as in chronic bronchitis which destroys many alveoli. Or there may be insufficient hemoglobin to combine with the amount of oxygen available, as in anemia. In diseases of the lung where portions of the lung become nonfunctional, there is a decrease in the amount of oxygen because of the decrease in total lung surface. A thickening of the walls of the alveoli and capillaries, caused by excessive fat deposits, also impairs oxygen supply, through impaired oxygen transference.

During normal breathing, which is usually somewhat shallow, the average amount of air taken in is about 500 cubic centimeters. Of this only about 20 percent is oxygen and about .03 percent is carbon dioxide. Only about 350 cc. of the 500 cc. actually reaches the lungs, since much is lost initially. By breathing very heavily, it is possible to inhale about 2500 cc. of air and thus increase the intake of oxygen, but respiration, like every process of the body, can only take place if energy is being synthesized from the burning of oxygen and glucose, and a higher level of oxidation is required when breathing deeply.

Thus, we see yet again that the functions of the body are essentially interlocking and interdependent. Although the body can adapt itself to the loss of certain tissues, the essential functions of respiration, digestion and assimilation, elimination, circulation of the blood and the cellular activity of the brain are all dependent on each other and truly cannot be studied in isolation. In order to survive, the patterns which the body has built up in the course of evolution must remain constant. As with all biological systems, the cells and tissues of the human body and brain must maintain their internal environment in a steady state.

It is surprising how little is still known of what constitutes this ideal steady state. However, by studying the system we can gain an insight into what our needs are and how we must deal with those needs in the future and how far we will be able to adapt, if that is possible, to a changing environment.

Bibliography

Afinson, Christian B.—*The Molecular Basis of Evolution* (New York: Wiley, 1969)

Afzelius, Bjorn (trans. Birgit H. Satir)—*Anatomy of the Cell* (Chicago: University of Chicago Press, 1966)

Azimov, Isaac—*The Human Body: Its Structure and Operation* (New York: Signet Science Library, 1971)

Babkin, B.P.—*Secretory Mechanism of Digestive Glands* (New York: Paul Hoeber, 1971)

Beadle, George and Muriel—*The Language of Life* (New York: Doubleday, 1971)

Bloom, William and Fawcett, Don—*Textbook of Histology* (Philadelphia: W.B. Saunders, 8th ed., 1962)

Borek, Ernest—*The Atoms Within Us* (New York: Columbia University Press, 1961)

Borek, Ernest—*The Code of Life* (New York: Columbia University Press, 1965)

Bonner, John Tyler—*The Ideas of Biology* (New York: Harper, 1962)

Boyer, P.D., Lardy, H.A. and Myerback, Karl (eds.) —*The Enzymes* (New York: Academic Press, 2nd ed., 8 vols., 1963)

Brachet, Jean and Mirsky, Alfred E.—*The Cell: Biochemistry, Physiology, Morphology* (New York: Academic Press, 5 vols., 1959-61)

Carles, Jules (trans. Francis Huxley)—*The Origins of Life* (New York: Walker, 1963)

Carpenter, Bruce H.—*Molecular and Cell Biology* (Belmont, California: Dickinson, 1967)

Colowick, S.P. and Kaplan, N.O. (eds.)—*Methods in Enzymology* (New York: Academic Press, 2 vols., 1955-67)

Crick, Francis—*Of Molecules and Men* (Seattle: University of Washington Press, 1966)

Davenport, H.W.—*Physiology of the Digestive Tract: Year Book of Medical Publishers* (Chicago: 1961, 1966)

Davis, Adele—*Let's Eat Right to Keep Fit* (New York: Signet, 1970)

Dixon, M. and Webb, E.C.—*Enzymes* (New York: Academic Press, 1964)

Friedman, M.—*Parthenogenesis of Coronary Artery Disease* (New York: McGraw-Hill, 1969)

Frisch, Karl von (trans. James M. Openheimer)—*Biology* (New York: Harper & Row, 1964)

Gaebler, Oliver H. (ed.)—*Enzymes: Units of Biological Structure and Function: Henry Ford Hospital International Symposium* (New York: Academic Press, 1966)

Galton, Lawrence—*The Silent Disease: Hypertension* (New York: Crown, 1973)

Gregory, R. A.—*Secretory Mechanisms of the Gastro-Intestinal Tract* (London: Arnold, 1962)

Guttfreund, H.—*An Introduction to the Study of Enzymes* (New York: Wiley, 1965)

Guyton, A.—*Textbook of Medical Physiology* (Philadelphia: W. B. Saunders, 1961)

Hardin, Garrett—*Biology: Its Principles and Implications* (San Francisco: W.H. Freeman, 1961)

Harrow, Benjamin and Mazur, Abraham—*Textbook in Biochemistry* (Philadelphia: W. B. Saunders, 1966)

Henahan, John F.—*Men and Molecules* (New York: Crown, 1966)

Jevons, F.R.—*The Biochemical Approach to Life* (London: Allen and Unwin, 1964)

Jerzy Glass, George B.—*Introduction to Gastrointestinal Physiology* (Englewood Cliffs, N.J.: Prentice-Hall, 1968)

Kendrew, John C.—*The Thread of Life* (Cambridge: Harvard University Press, 1966)

Lewis, Howard R. and Marta E.—*Psychosomatics* (New York: Viking, 1972)

Lewis, Paul and Rubinstein, David—*The Human Body* (New York: Bantam, 1971)

Locke, David M.—*Enzymes: The Agents of Life* (New York: Crown, 1969)

Loewy, A. and Siekevitz, P.—*Cell Structure and Function* (New York: Holt, 1965)

Maddox, John—*Revolution in Biology* (New York: Macmillan, 1964)

Magee, D.F.—*Gastrointestinal Physiology* (Springfield, Ill.: Charles C. Thomas, 1962)

Mercer, E.H.—*Cells: Their Structure and Function* (New York: Doubleday Anchor Natural History Library, 1962)

Munro, H.N. and Allison, J.B. (eds.)—*Mammalian Protein Metabolism* (New York: Academic Press, 2 vols., 1964)

Null, Gary and Steve—*The Complete Handbook of Nutrition* (New York: Robert Speller and Sons, 1972)

Rodale, J.I.—*The Complete Book of Food and Nutrition* (Emmaus, Penn.: Rodale Books, Inc., 1967)

Schulz, H.W. (ed.)—*Food Enzymes: Symposium on Foods, Oregon State College* (Westport, Conn.: Avi, 1960)

Smith, C.U.M.—*The Architecture of the Body* (London: Faber and Faber, 1964)

Smith, Ella Thea—*Exploring Biology* (New York: Harcourt Brace Jovanovich, 1959)

Spratt, N.—*Introduction to Cell Differentiation* (New York: Reinhold, 1966)

Strauss, Bernard S.—*An Outline of Chemical Genetics* (Philadelphia: W.B. Saunders, 1960)

Vogel, A.—*The Liver* (Teufen, Switzerland: Bioforce-Verlag, 1962)

Wade, Carlson—*Helping Your Health with Enzymes* (New York: Arc Books, 1966)

Wallace, Bruce—*Chromosomes, Giant Molecules and Evolution* (New York: Norton, 1966)

Watson, George—*Nutrition and Your Mind: The Psychochemical Response* (New York: Harper & Row, 1972)

Watson, J.D.—*Molecular Biology of the Gene* (New York: W.A. Benjamin Inc., 1965)

Webb, J. Leyden—*Enzyme and Metabolic Inhibitors* (New York: Academic Press, 3 vols., 1966)

White, Abraham, Handler, Philip and Smith, Emil—*Principles of Biochemistry* (New York: McGraw-Hill, 1973)

Wohl, M.G. and Goodhart, R.S. (eds.)—*Modern Nutrition in Health and Disease* (Philadelphia: Lea and Feibigger, 1960)

Index

A

adenosine triphosphate (ATP), 124
Akatsu, K., 102
All-India Institute for Mental Health (Bangalore), 101
All-India Institute of Medical Sciences (New Delhi), 101
alpha frequency (of brain), 82, 84, 87, 88-89
American Heart Association, The, 38
Anand, B.K., 101, 102
appendix (and digestive system), 133
Arkay, Arnold A., 47
arthritis, and fasting, 23
assimilation, 44, 130; *see also* digestive system
astrocytes, 143
Avicenna, 19

and automatic learning, 80; and the brain, 83-86; and behavior modification, 87; and hypertension, 90; importance of instruction in, 92; and knowledge of self, 93
blood, in digestion, 138-39; circulation of, 139-40
blood diseases, and fasting, 23
blood pressure, 140-42; and automatic nervous system, 142
Bogen, J. E. 85
Borgen, Joseph, 85
Bosse, Therese, 101
brain, and fasting, 55-62; and biofeedback, 83-86
brain waves, 81-82; *see also* alpha frequency, beta frequency, delta frequency, theta frequency
breathing, control of, 146
Brehner, Jasper, 90
Budzynski, Thomas, 91

B

Bagchi, B. K., 101
Baltimore City Hospital, 91
Benedict, F. G., 20
Benoit, R. C., 67
Benson, Herbert, 90, 91, 106, 107, 109
Berger, Hans, 81, 82
beta frequency (of brain), 82
biofeedback, 77-94; use of artificial respirator in, 80;

C

Carlson, A. J., 20, 21
Carlstrom, S. 49, 66
cells, 119-21; structure of, 119-20, functioning of, 120-21; *see also* nerve cells
cellubar respiration, 56-58
Childe, C. M., 20
China, G. S., 102
Christy, Aimee, 90
circulatory system, 139-40